ORACLE: Building High Performance Online Systems

JWu

Books from QED

Database

- Migrating to DB2
- DB2: The Complete Guide to Implementation and Use
- DB2 Design Review Guidelines
- DB2: Maximizing Performance of Online Production Systems
- Embedded SQL for DB2: Application Design and Programming
- SQL for DB2 and SQL/DS Application Developers
- Using DB2 to Build Decision Support Systems
- The Data Dictionary: Concepts and Uses
- Logical Data Base Design
- Entity-Relationship Approach to Logical Data Base Design
- Database Management Systems: Understanding and Applying Database Technology
- Database Machines and Decision Support Systems: Third Wave Processing
- IMS Design and Implementation Techniques
- Repository Manager/MVS: Concepts, Facilities and Capabilities
- How to Use ORACLE SQL*PLUS
- ORACLE: Building High Performance of Online Systems
- ORACLE Design Review Guidelines
- Using ORACLE to Build Decision Support Systems
- Understanding Data Pattern Processing: The Key to Competitive Advantage
- Developing Client/Server Aplications in an Architected Environment

Systems Engineering

- Quality Assurance for Information Systems: Methods, Tools, and Techniques
- Handbook of Screen Format Design
- Managing Software Projects: Selecting and Using PC-Based Project Management Systems
- The Complete Guide to Software Testing
- A User's Guide for Defining Software Requirements
- A Structured Approach to Systems Testing
- Storyboard Prototyping: A New Approach to User Requirements Analysis
- The Software Factory: Managing Software Development and Maintenance
- Data Architecture: The Information Paradigm
- Advanced Topics in Information Engineering
- Software Engineering with Formal Metrics

Management

- Introduction to Data Security and Controls
- CASE: The Potential and the Pitfalls

Management (cont'd)

- Strategic and Operational Planning for Information Services
- Information Systems Planning for Competitive Advantage
- How to Automate Your Computer Center: Achieving Unattended Operations
- Ethical Conflicts in Information and Computer Science, Technology, and Business
- Mind Your Business: Managing the Impact of End-User Computing
- Controlling the Future: Managing Technology-Driven Change
- The UNIX Industry: Evolution, Concepts, Architecture, Applications, and Standards

Data Communications

- Designing and Implementing Ethernet Networks
- Network Concepts and Architectures
- Open Systems: The Guide to OSI and its Implementation

IBM Mainframe Series

- CSP: Mastering Cross System Product
- CICS/VS: A Guide to Application Debugging
- MVS COBOL II Power Programmer's Desk Reference
- VSE COBOL II Power Programmer's Desk Reference
- CICS Application and System Programming: Tools and Techniques
- QMF: How to Use Query Management Facility with DB2 and SQL/DS
- DOS/VSE: Introduction to the Operating System
- DOS/VSE: CICS Systems Programming
- DOS/VSE/SP Guide for Systems Programming: Concepts, Programs, Macros, Subroutines
- Advanced VSE System Programming Techniques
- Systems Programmer's Problem Solver
- VSAM: Guide to Optimization and Design
- MVS/JCL: Mastering Job Control Language
- MVS/TSO: Mastering CLISTS
- MVS/TSO: Mastering Native Mode and ISPF
- REXX in the TSO Environment

Programming

- C Language for Programmers
- VAX/VMS: Mastering DCL Commands and Utilities
- The PC Data Handbook: Specifications for Maintenance, Repair, and Upgrade of the IBM/PC, PS/2 and Compatibles
- UNIX C Shell Desk Reference

ORACLE: Building High Performance Online Systems

W.H. Inmon

QED Information Sciences, Inc.
Wellesley, Massachusetts

QED Plaza
P.O. Box 181
Wellesley, MA 02181

Library of Congress Catalog Number: 89-10295
International Standard Book Number: 0-89435-302-0

Printed in the United States of America
91 10 9 8 7 6 5

Library of Congress Cataloging-in-Publication Data

Inmon, William H.
ORACLE : building high performance online systems / W.H. Inmon.
p. cm.
Bibliography: p.
Includes index.
ISBN 0-89435-302-0
1. Data base management. 2. ORACLE (Computer system)
3. On-line data processing. I. Title.
QA76.9.D3I544 1989
005.75′65—dc20

To Robin Sacks

Contents

Chapter 3 Conceptual Data Base Design—Normalization 37

Chapter 4 Conceptual Data Base Design—Denormalization 47

Chapter 5 Physical Data Base Design in ORACLE 65

Preface

ORACLE's data base product is a powerful tool with many capabilities. The possibilities and environments for using ORACLE are so numerous that ORACLE can be used by the end user, the programmer, the manager, the decision support analyst, and the information center analyst. Indeed, ORACLE has so many options that it can be the DBMS to suit nearly all the processing needs for a very wide spectrum of users. There is one very special usage of ORACLE that is the focus of this book—as a tool for production, online applications. It is recognized that ORACLE has many other legitimate uses that will not be covered by this book. Instead, the focus will be almost entirely on the issues of production, online processing.

The issues of production, online application processing begin with performance and availability. Performance refers, of course, to the amount of time required for a user to complete a transaction. Availability refers to the amount of time the system is up and running. In the production, online environment when the system either does not perform well or is unavailable, no other facets of the system matter. Consequently, the discipline that is required of the designer to achieve high performance and availability takes precedence over other features of ORACLE.

Online performance centers around the physical I/Os required to support the processing of online systems. The central issues of performance will naturally focus on the minimization and the effective use of I/Os.

I/Os are minimized by the proper construction of the production environment, by proper system design, and by proper tuning of the system once constructed. This book takes the philosophy that:

- If the online production environment is not properly constructed, then no amount of sound design or tuning will achieve, in the long run, adequate performance.
- If the application is not designed properly, then no amount of tuning will achieve, in the long run, adequate performance.
- After the production, online environment has been properly constructed and the application has been properly designed, then tuning the application provides the fine touches to enhance online performance.

The discussions throughout this book reflect the philosophy of creating good performance in the structured manner described.

This book is for application designers, system programmers, data base administrators, data administrators, project managers, consultants, managers of ORACLE production projects—in short, anyone interested in good performance and high system availability for production systems in the online environment. It discusses the following main subjects:

- Some of the salient aspects of ORACLE and environmental considerations relevant to performance and availability.
- ORACLE data base design and transaction design considerations. Discussion of some detailed technical considerations and batch window considerations.
- Transaction and program design for performance and availability.
- Specialized topics, such as processing, testing, extract processing, and so forth.

One of the problems of any technically oriented book is the relationship of the material in the book to the release of software. This book is current to release 6.0 of ORACLE. Many of the system considerations are directly relevant to the specifics of the release; however, most of the design concepts discussed in application design and the establishment of the online environment are generally applicable to any release of ORACLE.

This book is not a replacement for the basic manuals and materials that describe the mechanics of ORACLE. Those subjects are more than adequately discussed in the literature and are mentioned in the bibliography. Instead, this book assumes that the reader has at least a working knowledge of ORACLE and is interested not in the mechanics but in actually achieving results with ORACLE in an on-line mode.

ACKNOWLEDGMENTS

Contributing materially to this effort were the following:

Gary Dodge
Tom Devane
Margot Levy, American Management Systems
J D Welch, PacTel Cellular

Sincere thanks to all.
WHI 8/1/89

CHAPTER 1

ORACLE—An Overview

THE PRODUCTION ENVIRONMENT

The production environment is typified by much processing, lots of data, and a need for quick response time. Thus, there is always contention for resources inside ORACLE and the operating systems on which ORACLE runs. Given that there are only a finite amount of resources to go around in the production environment, it is assumed that system allocation resource decisions belong in the domain of the systems programmer. Other decisions belong in the domain of the application designer. This means that application designers and data base designers should not make assumptions about what will be in memory during the design process.

Some basic assumptions about the production environment that this book makes follow:

- The reader understands the very fundamental differences between the batch, online, and the interactive environments. If the reader does not understand the difference between the interactive and the online environment then it is suggested that he or she read no further until the differences are clearly spelled out and understood. The design techniques for each of the three environments are very different. This book is about the online environment and what is required to make it run successfully. Any other considerations about the interactive and the batch environments are incidental to the performance and success of the online environment.

- Most online, production processing involves update or update intent. That large amounts of read-only processing are possible in the online production environment is not an assumption that can normally be made, even though on occasions read-only processing can be done.
- Given the contention for resources that is found in the online, production environment, it CANNOT be assumed that much in buffer processing will occur. In some cases there actually will be much in buffer processing occurring, and performance will be accordingly good. But in the more general case, this is not a valid assumption to be made by the data base designer. The data base designer is preempting the domain of the systems programmer when the assumption is made that data will be held in the buffer for any length of time. Only the barest of assumptions can be made, such as the high probability of in-buffer processing of clustered data. ANY other assumptions about in-buffer processing are invalid for the online, production environment.
- The nature of production data bases is volume. It is assumed that there will be *much* data to be managed and manipulated in the online, production environment.

DESIGN CONSIDERATIONS

The first step in designing production systems under ORACLE is understanding the basic structures and components of ORACLE and how they relate. The introductory chapters are for the reader who has had little or no introduction to the ORACLE data base product. The reader who has been introduced to the ORACLE product should skip these introductory chapters and proceed directly to the chapters on data base design.

The first introductory section covers columns, rows, tables, storage structures, and indexes.

BASIC DATA BASE DESIGN

The basic data base design components of ORACLE with which the application designer needs to become familiar are:

- The column
- The row
- The table

There are other components of data storage that the designer needs to be aware of, even though in the process of transforming requirements into a design, these levels of storage are of secondary importance. These other levels are:

- The tablespace
- The segment
- The data base

After data has been organized into tables, the next major decision facing the designer is the indexing of the data. Indexes are built on keys, a column, or columns used to identify a row in a table. There can be many kinds of indexing strategies in ORACLE.

This first section will focus on the basic storage constructs that the designer needs to know.

Columns

The most basic unit of information in ORACLE is the column. The column in other data base management systems is known as an element or a field. The column indicates to ORACLE that all data defined to be in the column is of the same type and possesses the same physical characteristics.

As a simple example of a column, the designer may want to specify:

- Partno
- Desc
- Unitmeas
- Qtyonhnd

The columns that have been specified are PARTNO or part number for a manufacturing process, DESC or description of the part number in the manufacturing process, UNITMEAS or unit of measure of the part number, and QTYONHND or quantity on hand of the part number involved in the manufacturing process.

Each part number would have a separate occurrence. For example, each of the following might be a separate occurrence of a part number:

```
Partno▒QXZ009
       WSX008
       SEZ097
       ESW090
       ......
       ......
```

And for each occurrence of a part number, there might be an occurrence of description:

```
■ Partno – QXZ009 Desc – cam shaft
           WSX008        rocker arm
           SEZ097        idler
           ESW090        exhaust manifold
           ......        ................
           ......        ................
```

One of the features of a column is its physical characteristic. While the column is still being discussed in the early stages of design, there may be no physical attributes assigned to it. But at the moment that the column is defined to ORACLE, a physical attribute must be assigned. There can be one and only one physical attribute assigned to each column.

The designer needs to take a fair amount of care in assigning physical attributes to columns because, while the physical attribute may be changed after the data base is built, it is not desirable to make such changes frequently. There is a fair amount of work that needs to be done to physically change an attribute in most cases. In a few cases, such as lengthening a column or dropping NOT NULL, only the dictionary needs to be changed, which does not require a great number of resources.

PHYSICAL ATTRIBUTES The physical attributes that can be assigned to a column are:

- CHAR or VARCHAR (they are interchangeable)
- NUMBER
- DATE
- LONG
- RAW
- LONG RAW

Each of the types of physical attributes will be briefly described here. For an in-depth discussion, refer to ORACLE documentation.

CHAR or VARCHAR is how alphanumeric characters are specified. There is no difference between CHAR and VARCHAR. The maximum number of characters that can be specified in any assignment is 255. In later releases, CHAR will specify a fixed-length column.

NUMBER is used to store numeric values. A typical usage of the NUMBER assignment is to specify precision and scale of the values. For example, NUMBER (10,2) indicates that the column has ten digits in total and the last two of those digits are after the decimal point. NUMBER can also be used to specify floating point values.

DATE is used to specify a date field. Each DATE field is seven bytes long. The seven bytes are used to specify:

- Century
- Year
- Month
- Day
- Hour
- Minute
- Second

LONG is used to specify long strings of variable data up to 65,535 bytes in length. (Note: this varies by operating system.) LONG specifies a sequentially packed series of characters, with no structure implied.

RAW is the specification (like CHAR) for bytes of data, except that the data specified in RAW is not assumed to be in any character format.

LONG RAW is like RAW, except that more data is specified.

ADDING PHYSICAL CHARACTERISTICS TO COLUMNS After the columns are decided on, their physical characteristics must be assigned before they can be defined to ORACLE. The following is an example of a typical assignment of physical attributes.

- Partno char (25)
- Desc char (50)
- Unitmeas char (1)
- Qtyonhnd number (11,0)

An option for columns is NOT NULL. The default assignment for a column is NULL. When a column can contain null values, there may be no value assigned for a given occurrence of the column.

Row

A row is made up of columns. Each row contains the same column types with different occurrences of data. An example serves best to explain a row.

```
        COLA           COLB        COLC             COLD
row1    partno    .    desc    .   unitmeas    .    qtyonhnd
row2    partno    .    desc    .   unitmeas    .    qtyonhnd
row3    partno    .    desc    .   unitmeas    .    qtyonhnd
row4    partno    .    desc    .   unitmeas    .    qtyonhnd
row5    partno    .    desc    .   unitmeas    .    qtyonhnd
        ......         ....        ........         ........
rown    ......         ....        ........         ........
```

The example shows that rows go across the page and contain one occurrence of partno, desc, unitmeas, and qtyonhnd. The columns go down the page and contain one type of data. Of course, the example given shows data values symbolically.

Actual occurrences of data would look like:

	COLA	COLB	COLC	COLD
row1	QXZ008	rocker arm	P	92
row2	WSX009	idler	P	0
row3	SEZ097	cam shaft	B	125
row4	ESW090	manifold	C	4
row5	RTY870	H valve	P	35
....	......	....	.	.
rown	WED097	PAV valve	P	126

In row 1, the part number is QXZ008. The description of part number QXZ008 is "rocker arm." The unit of measure for QXZ008 is "p," or by the part. The number of units on hand is 92.

Tables

Columns are grouped together to form tables. The collection of rows that has been shown is called a table.

The application designer, then, is interested in three aspects of ORACLE, as far as data base design is concerned:

- What are the columns
- What are the rows
- What are the tables

In addition, the application designer needs to specify the physical attributes of the columns.

Other Storage Structures

ORACLE has physical storage structures other than those discussed. The application designer needs to be aware that those structures exist, but they do not play a large role in the design of the application. Instead, as the application heads towards implementation, the data base administrator assigns those storage components to the design.

The other storage components that ORACLE has are:

- Segments
- Tablespaces
- Databases

The structure of the storage components of ORACLE can be expressed as:

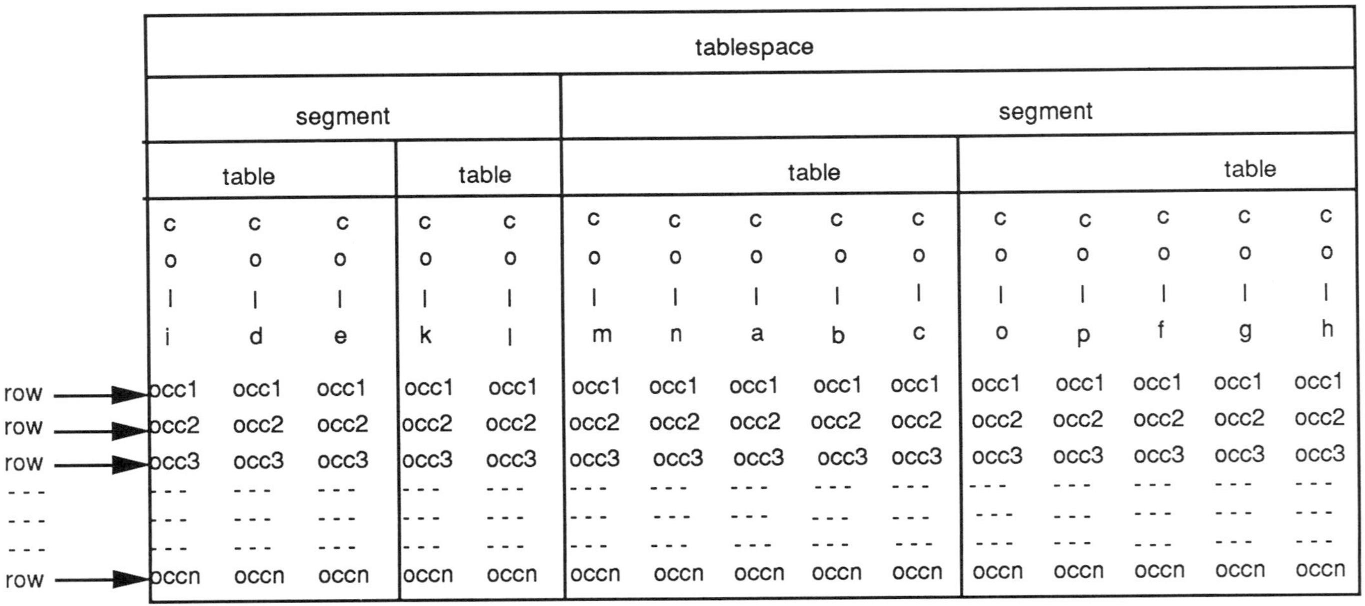
tablespace
segment
segment
table
table
table
table
col i, col d, col e, col k, col l, col m, col n, col a, col b, col c, col o, col p, col f, col g, col h
row
row
row
row
occ1
occ2
occ3
occn

However, there is a higher order of arranging data than at the tablespace level. That order can be expressed by:

```
 . . . . . . . . . .
tbspc         .
              .
tbspc         .
          database
tbspc         .
              .
tbspc         .
 . . . . . . . . . .
```

The diagrams show that occurrences of data are found in columns. The occurrences are grouped together into columns to form rows. Rows of data form tables. Tables of data form index or data segments. Index or data segments form tablespaces. And tablespaces form data bases.

INDEXES An index is a special data structure that is used for the direct access of data. Consider a table, as shown, without an index.

ENGINE PARTS TABLE

	COLA	COLB	COLC	COLD
row1	QWS345	rocker arm	P	98
row2	ERF560	cam shaft	P	108
row3	TYG009	boiler plate	B	97
row4	TRS080	ex. manifold	C	0
row5	WHI064	idler control	P	128
....	......	....	.	....
....	......	....	.	....
rown	RTE099	wheel shift	P	1006

Suppose it was desired to find a single part, say part TRS080. The programmer may specify that part TRS080 is to be found when there is no index. But that means that ORACLE will have to search through the entire table, part by part, until part TRS080 is located. Even after TRS080 is located, the search will continue in case there are more than one part with the same part number.

If the table is very small, or if the search is done very infrequently, then searching through the entire table, row by row, may not be a bad thing to do. But for most tables that will be found in the production environment that contain more than a small amount of data, such a search will consume many resources.

A better way to find part TRS080 is to create an index. Then, when it is desired to locate the part, ORACLE will use the index to determine where the part is. In such a fashion the bulk of data in the table will not have to be searched row by row. This type of searching is very efficient.

An index, then, is a very small, very compact data structure (a B-tree structure) table managed directly by ORACLE that contains the value of the column(s) being indexed and a pointer to the physical location of the row. The index is ordered in the sequence of the values of the column(s) being indexed. It is generally much more efficient to search an index for a specific value than it is to search the table, row by row, under normal circumstances.

As an example of what a simple index may look like for the PARTS table that has been used as the example above, the following is what might be expected:

PARTS INDEX

PART	LOCATION
......	....
ERF060	block 9067
......	....
......	....
QWS345	block 1054
RTE099	block 0097
......	....
TRS080	block 0868
TYG009	block 9067
......	....
WHI064	block 1906
......	....

The index contains only the key value and the location of the row where the key value and non-key columns that relate to the key value can be found. No other information, such as unit of measure, is found.

There are many options that apply to indexes. One option is that any column may be indexed. Another is that an index may be specified to be UNIQUE. When an index is specified to be unique, no two values may be inserted that are the same. For example, without an index specifying that the column PART be UNIQUE, is it possible to insert a row with a value for part of "TYG009"? Of course it is. There is no reason why the PARTS table cannot contain two rows that have a part valued as "TYG009."

But if the column PART is indexed and the index is specified as UNIQUE, then as the table exists as shown, only one row can ever exist with a value of PART equalling "TYG009."

Another useful design option using indexes occurs where two or more columns need to be concatenated in order to create an index. ORACLE allows columns to be concatenated and indexed. The concatenated key may contain up to 16 columns and be up to 255 bytes in length, although such large concatenated keys are rarely found. For example, suppose that for the PARTS table that has been discussed, it was desired to concatenate two columns: the description column—COLB, and the unit of measure column—COLC.

The following index could be created:

DESCRIPTION, UNIT OF MEASURE INDEX

DESC	U/M	LOCATION
....	.	....
boiler plate	B	block 1067
boiler plate	B	block 0912
boiler plate	P	block 1097
....	.	....
cam shaft	.	block 0097
....	.	....
ex. manifold	B	block 8097
ex. manifold	C	block 1067
....	.	....
....	.	....

Of course, the concatenation could occur in the reverse order, where unit of measure is the first column to be concatenated and description is the second column to be concatenated. If the order were reversed, the result might look like:

UNIT OF MEASURE, DESCRIPTION INDEX

U/M	DESCRIPTION	LOCATION
A	choke	block 1045
A	idler	block 1099
A	rocker arm	block 0012
.	. . . .	. . . .
B	boiler plate	block 0035
B	boiler plate	block 9087
B	gaskets—type A	block 0018
B	gaskets—type V	block 1099
.	. . . .	. . . .
.	. . . .	. . . .

Even though the two indexes—the DESCRIPTION, UNIT OF MEASURE index and the UNIT OF MEASURE, DESCRIPTION index—have exactly the same contents, they are in a different order. Depending on the activity, a search through one index may be much more efficient than a search through the other index.

Not only can indexes be specified for any column and over multiple columns, but as many indexes as desired may be specified. For all practical purposes, there are no limits on how many indexes may be specified.

At first glance it may appear that using an index will greatly improve efficiency of processing, and in general this is true. But there is a tradeoff the application designer must make, which is that, while indexes enhance efficiency of processing when it comes time to access data, indexes increase overhead in the update and loading of data. Furthermore, the overhead incurred is not a small one. So the enhancement of performance in the accessing of data is balanced by the overhead in the updating and loading of data.

In general, the more indexes there are, the worse performance becomes as the tables are updated. As a rule, a table should have from two to three indexes per table. There will be exceptions to this rule. Some tables will be so small that no indexes are required. Other tables will be accessed in such a way that it is mandatory that multiple indexes be built. But on the average, from two to three indexes per table should be the norm.

To understand how loading and update affect an index, consider some simple activities. For example, what action is required when part

RTY657 is loaded in to the PARTS table. The system must go through the motions of loading the part into its table, and that requires a certain amount of overhead. But the index must be loaded as well. With the insertion of the row, all indexes that reference the row must be altered. In addition, it may not be as simple as placing the value "RTY657" in the index.

There is every chance that physically there may be no space for the insertion of the value into the index and where the order of the index can be maintained. Remember that while the row of data can be placed in any block, the index entry needs to be placed in one and only one place in a particular block. And if there is no space available in that block, then the system must go through considerable overhead in making space available.

Loading data does not entail quite the same complexity as updating data. But suppose there are six indexes on a table. As each row is loaded, the system requires that seven entries of data be placed into a table or an index. Furthermore, the order of the indexes is most likely other than the sequence in which the rows are being loaded.

For these reasons, the overhead of updating and loading indexes must be balanced against the potential performance gains that are possible in using the index to access data.

SOME EXCEPTIONS The general rule is that indexes save performance for the access of data, but that is not always the case. Wholesale access of a data base through an index can greatly harm performance. The section that discusses I/O will further elaborate on this topic.

Another exception is the "secondary" or the "sparse" index. This type of index is built at the application level and should be in the repertoire of every application designer. The sparse index is not an indexing option directly supported by ORACLE, but it is such an important option and has so many potential uses that the application designer should understand what it is and when it is to be used.

Consider the PARTS table that has been discussed. Suppose it was desired to access all parts on a regular basis that have a unit of measure of "T." In other words, the production control analyst desires to find out information about all parts whose unit of measure is in a tin (e.g., U/M = "T").

One way to find all those parts is to scan the entire PARTS table data base. But this requires looking at every single part in the table and is quite wasteful of resources. Another way to accomplish the same task is to build an index on the UNIT OF MEASURE column. This works quite nicely, except there are many parts that have a unit of measure other than "T" and maintaining the index just for accessing all parts whose unit of measure is "T" is not justified.

The application designer then has a dilemma. The table is too large to be scanned frequently, and the index that is required is not used enough to justify its existence. The answer is to build what is referred to as a "sparse" index.

A sparse index is built only at the application level. In the example, the designer would build a UNIT OF MEASURE–"T" table, which would contain values only of parts that had a unit of measure that equaled "T". The table would contain only a very few columns, such as PART and perhaps DESCRIPTION. The table would be indexed, as shown

"T" INDEX		U/M "T" TABLE		
PART	LOCATION	PART	DESCRIPTION	LOCATION
FRT675	block 001	OPI090	carb setter	block 0098
GFE009	block 002	FRT675	thermostat	block 0097
OPI090	block 001	OPN998	fuel line	block 9822
OPK099	block 001	OPK099	gas gauge	block 8711
OPM001	block 002	OPM001	gasket # 0019	block 7723
OPN998	block 001	GFE009	oil filter	block 3343
OPN999	block 003	OPN999	wing nut # 023	block 3346
......	....	......	....	....

The relationship between the "T" index, the U/M "T" table, and the PARTS table is shown:

"T" INDEX	U/M "T" TABLE	PARTS TABLE
3400 entries	3400 entries	267,000 entries

The "T" index points into the U/M "T" table. There are only 3,400 entries in both the index and the table. The U/M "T" table contains only the key of the rows whose U/M value is "T." It is efficient for the application designer to access all parts with a value of "T" now because there is no need to scan the entire PARTS table and because there is no need to create an index on the UNIT OF MEASURE column for the PARTS table.

While there are many advantages to a sparse index, there are some corresponding disadvantages. One disadvantage is that the "T" index and the U/M "T" table have to be loaded and kept up to date. Every time a part with a value of "T" is added or deleted from the PARTS table, a corresponding deletion or addition is required in the index and the sparse index.

Another disadvantage of a sparse index is that the integrity of the index is maintained by application code. There is the chance that an application may not be built correctly and that upon execution the sparse index will not be built and maintained properly.

For these reasons, it is wise to build sparse indexes on columns that are very stable or for which there are relatively few entries.

Furthermore, if the designer has chosen to include tables of other than key information in the sparse table, such as DESCRIPTION, then every time values change in the PARTS table, the sparse index must be updated.

SUMMARY

In this introductory chapter, the following basic storage concepts have been introduced:

- columns
- rows
- tables

In addition, the underlying types of data that are available to the designer have been discussed. Other types of data structures are brought to the application developer's attention.

Indexes—what they are, how they are used, and what options are available—have been discussed, along with the advantages and disadvantages of using an index. The overhead of loading and maintenance is balanced against the utility of accessing data.

QUESTIONS: ORACLE—AN OVERVIEW

1. The lowest unit of storage in ORACLE is:
   a. the column
   b. the row
   c. the table
   d. a field
2. Other levels of data storage in ORACLE are (choose all that apply):
   a. the tablespace
   b. the segment
   c. the file
   d. the data base
   e. the record
3. Data is normally accessed through ______________ .
4. If data is accessed through other than an index, THE ENTIRE/SOME OF THE table must be reordered.
5. Searching entire tables is efficient (choose all that apply):
   a. never
   b. when there are few indexes
   c. when the table is small
   d. when there is a sparse index
   e. when only a few values populate the index
6. Different types of data MAY/MAY NOT populate a column.
7. Each column has a ______________ and a ______________.
8. Columns can be related to other columns. (T/F)
9. The physical attribute of a column MAY/MAY NOT be easily changed after implementation.
10. The physical attributes that are possible in ORACLE are (choose all that apply):
    a. CHAR, VARCHAR
    b. NUMBER
    c. DATE
    d. LONG
    e. RAW
    f. LONGRAW
11. There is a slight difference between CHAR and VARCHAR. (T/F)
12. A CHAR column can be up to ______________ bytes in length.

13. The two types of NUMBER are ______________ and ______________ .

14. Fixed-point numbers can have their ______________ and ______________ specified.

15. A DATE column is ______________ bytes in length.

16. LONG can store character strips up to ______________ bytes in length.

17. LONG CAN/CANNOT be used to store non-character data.

18. RAW can be used to store ANY/CHARACTER/ONLY NON-CHARACTER data.

19. LONGRAW can be used to store the same type of data as RAW. (T/F)

20. A column can have NONE/ONE/MANY physical attributes.

21. Any column may have the NULL option. (T/F)

22. Columns are grouped together to form ______________ .

23. All rows of the same type have the same columns defined for them. (T/F)

24. Two rows of the same type may have the same columns, but the columns are defined in different order. (T/F)

25. All rows of the same type have the same physical length. (T/F)

26. Rows combine to form a ______________ table.

27. The application designer is not terribly concerned with tablespaces, segments, and data bases. Those levels of storage are more the concern of the ______________ .

28. If a search is done infrequently, accessing data by means of a full data base scan MAY NOT BE/MAY BE/IS NEVER justified.

29. An index contains (choose all that apply):
   a. the key of the field being indexed
   b. other columns than the index
   c. the address of the occurrence of data
   d. concatenated columns
   e. CHAR data

30. An indexed value may be concatenated. (T/F)

31. An index MAY BE/MAY NOT BE/MUST BE specified.

32. If an index is UNIQUE, NULL MAY/MAY NOT/MUST BE specified.

33. If two indexes are created on the same columns, but the order of the columns is different, the indexes (choose all that apply):
a. will contain the same information
b. will be identical
c. will be in different order
d. will be very similar but not exactly the same
e. will have a different number of entries

34. The limit of the number of indexes a table may have is:
a. a system limitation
b. there is no limit
c. a practical limitation
d. no more than three

35. Accessing data by means of an index always increases the efficiency of accessing a table. (T/F)

36. The two overhead activities that are associated with an index are the ______________ of the index and the ______________ of the index.

37. Because of the overhead associated with an index, any table should have no more than ______________ or ______________ indexes.

38. It is more efficient to load an index:
a. as the table is being built
b. after the table is built

39. Upon insertion of a new row, the row can be placed ______________ and the index is placed ______________.

40. If there is no space to place data in an index, the choice is (choose all that apply):
a. simply do not allow the insertion
b. build the row but not the index
c. split the index block
d. there is always space in the index
e. insert the index entry wherever possible and "remember" that it could not be inserted.

41. Upon insertion of a row, ALL/SOME/A FEW/NONE of the indexes on the row must be updated.

42. Wholesale access to a table by means of an index on other than the primary key is a GOOD/BAD/SOMETIMES GOOD/USUALLY BAD idea.

43. A sparse index is built at the ______________ level.

44. A sparse index contains MORE/FEWER/ABOUT THE SAME entries as the table that it points into.
45. Scanning a sparse index is very efficient. (T/F)

CHAPTER 2

ORACLE—More Basics

The first chapter discussed columns, rows, and tables, as well as indexes. This chapter continues the introductory discussion of ORACLE, specifically keys, IOs, programs/SQL, utilities, online/batch processing, and relationships.

KEYS

A key is one or more columns that identify a row, either uniquely or non-uniquely. These columns are identified during conceptual design and then transformed into a key at physical design. Usually a key is indexed.

As a simple example of a key, consider the table for an insurance company.

INSURANCE POLICY TABLE

POLICY NO	NAME	TYPE	COVERAGE	EFF DATE
00021-a	Jones, Indiana	L	$100,000	12/12/48
00010	Drew, Nancy	H	$20,000	01/01/54
00450-a	Barrow, Clyde	L	$15,000	01/24/36
00450-b	Parker, Bonnie	L	$15,000	02/24/36
00350	Cerf, Bennett	L	$2,000,000	15/07/46
00135-a	Daly, John	L	$1,000,000	01/07/38
00897	Spade, Sam	H	$5,000	01/08/35

POLICY NO	NAME	TYPE	COVERAGE	EFF DATE
00013-a	Berle, Milton	L	$1,000,000	01/07/39
....	....	.	....	....
....	....	.	....	....

The analyst wishes to access the table often by policy number. A key is created on policy number by creating an index. Another analyst wishes to access the data by type of policy and coverage. Another key is created by concatenating those two columns and creating an index.

Assuming that policy number is unique, the key on policy number is likewise unique. Of course, the concatenated key on type of policy and coverage is not unique.

And, depending on the overhead required in the loading and maintenance of the key, as many indexes per table as desired can be created.

Strictly speaking, an index per key is not required. But given the size of production application data bases, regularly accessing a table by a column without an index is not a sound design practice.

Keys can generally be classified into two types: primary and secondary. A primary key is one that uniquely identifies a row, such as policy number in the example. Secondary keys are those that do not uniquely identify a row, such as the concatenated key on type of policy and coverage limit. While there can be only one policy number in the table, there may be many rows with the same type of policy and coverage limit. The notion of primary keys and secondary keys stems from the analysis done in the early phases of development.

CLUSTERING DATA

One of the best uses of keys is for the clustering of data. A table or tables can either be clustered once or not at all. Clustering refers to the physical placement of rows of data in the same physical location based on a common key value.

For example, suppose that in addition to the policy table that has been discussed, there was also a claims table, as shown:

INSURANCE CLAIMS TABLE

CLAIM	POLICY	DATE	AMOUNT	BY	SETTLED?
009a	00013-a	02/15/48	$10,890	Dahl, A.	Y
090s	00156	09/28/47	$156,784	Sales, S.	N

```
CLAIM POLICY    DATE     AMOUNT        BY        SETTLED?
234f 00014-b 09/30/39  $23,992 Capone, A.          Y

122f 01305   12/31/41 $430,000 Dillinger, J.       N

224f 00245   04/26/43  $13,676 Lorre, P.           Y

335j 00341-c 07/11/46   $1,000 Castro, F.          Y

............ ........ ........ ............        .
............ ........ ........ ............        .
```

Now suppose that both policy and claim information is accessed together very frequently. Processing must always go from one table to the next, looking for policies of the same value. In other words, processing looks for policy number xxxxx in the policy table. Then the processing looks for the same policy number—xxxxx—in the claims table.

Jumping from one table to the next requires much work of the system. Clustering can be used to physically colocate the same policy data in the same physical block from both tables.

Two types of information are stored in the same physical block of data, as shown:

```
BLOCK  DATA
  1    row for policy data, policy 00003-c
  2    row for policy data, policy 00004
  2    row for claims data, policy 00004
  3    row for policy data, policy 00006
  3    row for claims data, policy 00006
  3    row for claims data, policy 00006
  3    row for claims data, policy 00006
  4    row for policy data, policy 00010-a
  5    row for policy data, policy 00010-b
  6    row for policy data, policy 00011
  7    row for policy data, policy 00013
  7    row for claims data, policy 00013
  7    row for claims data, policy 00013
  8    row for policy data, policy 00015
       .....................................
       .....................................
```

Clustering of data is, then, a very powerful way to structure data for efficient access. There are some disadvantages to the physical clustering of data that the application designer should be aware of. The first (and most obvious disadvantage) is that a table can be clustered at most in one way. That is why it is very important to choose clustering options to optimize processing that occurs very frequently.

The second disadvantage of clustering is that it requires data management at the moment of insertion of new rows. For example, suppose BLOCK 24 is entirely full. And suppose that a new row—a row for policy 00456-a—is to be inserted into the block. Either the row cannot be inserted and the system must "remember" that there is data outside its block that in fact belongs there, or the row is inserted by "splitting" the block. When a block is split, another block of space is allocated that has no data in it. The new block has about half of the contents of the full block written into it. Then the full block has the data that has been written "erased," leaving room for the new row to be written. Needless to say, this data management work that is done "beneath the covers" requires a large amount of resources.

Yet another disadvantage of clustering occurs when there is a change in a key value. With clustering, the change in key values requires relocating data from one block to another.

There are two options ORACLE has that help to alleviate some of the difficulties of data management in the face of adding or updating data to a clustered table. They are the PCTFREE and PCTUSED options. The PCTFREE option specifies how much space inside a block needs to be left free for updates. The more free space that is left in each block, the less the chance of a data management problem as the table is being updated. The other parameter that is useful is PCTUSED, which indicates to ORACLE how much space in the block the analyst wishes to keep filled.

Thus, clustering is an option that can significantly enhance performance under the right conditions. However, the application designer must be fully aware of the limitations of clustering before the option is chosen.

I/OS

At the heart of performance of the system is the activity known as "I/O," which, stands for input/output operation. I/O occurs when the system must read or write data to or from external storage, such as DASD, or disk storage.

The more times the program does I/O, the worse performance gets. That is why the designer must contend with such things as indexes and clustering of data, because these design options can greatly reduce the amount of I/O the system must do in order to execute its applications.

Why does I/O present the bottleneck to performance that it does? I/O operates at mechanical speeds while the computer runs at electronic speeds. I/O operates in milliseconds while the computer operates in nanoseconds. And there is a difference of about three orders of magnitude between the two rates of processing.

To appreciate the importance of the difference in speeds, consider (analogically) an admittedly strange trip. A man boards a jet that can travel at about 600 miles per hour in Miami. He flies to New York's LaGuardia Airport. He gets off the jet and walks (at about six miles per hour) to Kennedy Airport, where he boards a plane for Midway Airport in Chicago. There he disembarks and walks to O'Hare Airport. At O'Hare he gets on another jet and flies to Dallas' Love Field. In Dallas he walks to the Dallas-Fort Worth Airport and boards another plane.

Now how would one improve the speed of the trip the man is making? Flying on a faster airplane would do little to improve the time needed for the journey. Instead, there are great savings to be made in either eliminating the need to stop in Chicago and Dallas, or if you have to stop in Chicago or Dallas, at least traveling by cab from one airport to the next once you are there. In other words, for the elapsed time for the trip there is much more time spent in walking between airports than there is in flying from one city to the next.

Now, a person would be strange if he or she took such an odd trip. But the computer goes on this same kind of trip every time a program is executed. The computer operates at the speed of a jet while I/O operates at the speed of a man walking.

Furthermore, the way computers execute instructions, one statement cannot execute until the previous one has successfully completed. Consider the very simple, very common sequence of instructions:

```
• • • • • • • • • • •
• • • • • • • • • • •
IF A = B
THEN ADD 50 TO C
ELSE
SUBTRACT 35 FROM B
```

```
READ FILE POLICY
IF POLICY > POLICY_HOLD
. . . . . . . . . . .
. . . . . . . . . . .
```

The amount of time it takes to go from an IF to a THEN, or from an ADD to a SUBTRACT is very short at electronic speeds. But consider the time that it takes to go from a READ to the following IF statement. It takes an eternity because the program must execute an I/O in order to get its hands on the data, before it can properly execute the IF statement. In other words, the IF statement cannot execute until it is presented with the proper data, and an I/O is required to get the proper data. And doing the I/O takes a long, long time, in terms relative to the computer's speed.

There is a difference in types of I/Os the designer should be aware of. Effective with Version 6, much I/O (especially WRITEs) is asynchronous to the transactions that cause it. Physical writes occur only at the point of a COMMIT. They are piggybacked in multi-user systems and require only writes of condensed log records. This efficiency of writes implies that the designer should be much more conscious of reads as an I/O-causing event.

Therefore, the crux of application design for production systems is to reduce or eliminate physical I/O wherever possible. The less I/O required, the more efficient the system in its execution.

There are two kinds of I/O: logical (or virtual) I/O and physical I/O. Physical I/O occurs when the system actually has to go out and fetch data from a mechanical device. Logical I/O occurs when the system has the data in the computer already and can satisfy the request for I/O without actually having to go out to a storage device. Of course, it is much faster to do a logical I/O than a physical I/O. But the application designer should not design a system based on the assumption that much or most of the I/O that is done will be logical. There are many good reasons for not making this important assumption, even though, on occasion, an application will execute when most of the I/O done is logical.

PROGRAMS/SQL

The logic that is executed and the instructions for execution are done by programs. A program is code specified by the programmer to carry out the business function specified by the application designer. The application code that is written directs the activities of the computer through an interface, or language known as SQL. SQL directs the data base management system to do specific activities against the data base, such as access data, insert data, delete data, and so forth.

ONLINE/BATCH PROCESSING

In general, the day is divided up into two periods: a "batch window" and the online peak-period processing. The online processing usually occurs during regular business working hours—typically Monday through Friday, from 8:30 A.M. to 4:30 P.M. During online processing, transactions are run. While transactions are run, response time is very good because people are waiting on the completion of the transaction in order to conduct their daily business. If a customer has to wait five seconds in order to conduct business, there is no problem. But if a customer has to wait five minutes to conduct the same item of business, he or she will soon find another establishment to do business with.

Thus, the orientation of processing during the peak period is toward the completion of many short transactions, each of which runs in a modest amount of time. These transactions are usually at the heart of the business of the enterprise. Because the system is so sensitive to response time during the running of transactions in peak-period processing, there is no opportunity to run longer-running programs.

The longer-running programs run at night, or at least after the peak period of transaction processing is complete. This time is called the "batch window." Most long-running programs, then, execute out of the way of the fast-running transactions. In addition, the batch window is the time many utility programs are executed. Back-up processing, reorganizations, monitoring of data, and so forth, all occur during this time frame.

Not all organizations have the luxury of having a well-defined batch window and peak-period transaction processing. The business of some organizations demands 24-hour-a-day transaction capabilities. In this case, special design techniques are required.

UTILITIES

The application designer should be aware that every data base requires its own utilities to be run. Some of the standard utilities are:

- Reorganization
- Recovery

- Loading
- Monitoring

Reorganization of data is done when the internal contents of the data base become disorganized or when there is a need to restructure the contents of the table. Recovery, including back-up activity, is done to insure that the integrity of data is maintained. Should an error occur in processing, backup and recovery insure that the error can be backed out without damaging the data base.

Loading of data occurs when the data base is initially built. At this time, indexes are built. Monitoring of data and data relationships occurs occasionally in order to determine how much data there is, what the status of a relationship is, and so forth.

The utilities are usually provided by ORACLE, although in some cases the application programmer may wish to build his or her own utilities.

RELATIONSHIPS

One of the most powerful features of a data base management system in general, and ORACLE in particular, is the ability to build and maintain relationships between tables of data. The relationships that can be built allow the application designer to translate the needs and structures of the business into a data base design.

Some of the more common relationships with which the application designer should become familiar are:

- 1:n relationship
- M:n relationship, using cross reference tables
- Recursive relationship

1:N Relationship

The most common relationship is the 1:n relationship. The 1:n relationship exists between two tables, A and B. Table A contains a key value—KEYA. Table B contains the same column, KEYA, as part of its data. Usually the primary key of table B is not the column KEYA. For a row to exist in table B, there must first exist the same key in table A. There is then a 1:n relationship between the data in table A and the data in table B based on the common column KEYA. The column KEYA in table B is often referred to as a "foreign" key.

As an example of a 1:n relationship, refer to the two tables discussed in clustering—the POLICY table, and the CLAIMS table. In order for the insurance company to have a claim brought against it, a policy first must exist. If no policy exists, then no claim can be considered. And any policy may have multiple (or no) claims brought against it. There is then a classical 1:n relationship between the POLICY and the CLAIMS tables.

POLICY	CLAIM
•••••••	••••••
00078-a	••••••
00078-b	00908q
•••••••	00909z
•••••••	00910x
00081	••••••
00083	01009s
00086	01109f
00086	01119d
00086	01189h
00086	01167i
•••••••	••••••
•••••••	••••••

M:N Relationship

A more complex type of relationship is the m:n relationship. In a simplistic sense, an m:n relationship is nothing more than two 1:n relationships that are put together. In fact, it is possible to implement an m:n relationship as two 1:n relationships. However, implementation is usually not done that way because building and managing the relationship becomes complex. There is always the possibility of a loss of meaning of the relationship when this simplistic approach is taken.

Another approach is to separate the relationships from the tables that contain the base data. This technique is often called using cross-reference tables. As an example of using cross-reference tables, suppose the POLICY and the CLAIMS tables have a somewhat different relationship than that described. Suppose a claim could go against not just one, but multiple policies. There could then be an m:n relationship between policies and claims. (In the previous discussion of the relationship it was assumed that a claim could go against only one policy.)

One way to implement this m:n relationship is to build two cross-reference tables. One cross-reference table shows the claims-to-policy relationship, and the other cross-reference table shows the policy-to-claims relationship. In addition, the base tables have their information concerning the relationship to each other stripped from them.

The result is four tables:

POLICY TABLE

POLICY NO	NAME	TYPE	COVERAGE	DATE
00014-a	Parton, Dolly	H	$1,000,000	08/12/86
00015-b	Ronstadt, L	C	$2,000,000	09/15/82
00017	Harris, E Lou	H	$100,000	08/15/87
00001	Nelson, William	H	$1,000,000	01/10/87
00023	Williams, Henry	C	$350,000	01/02/88
....	....	.	....	....
....	....	.	....	....

CLAIMS TABLE

CLAIM NO	DATE	AMOUNT	TYPE	SETTLED?
009a	01/15/89	$10,000	C	Y
008s	02/12/87	$125,000	D	N
007a	04/25/87	$1,000	D	Y
010x	06/30/88	$450,000	C	Y
....	....	....	.	.
....	....	....	.	.

CLAIMS-POLICY XREF

CLAIM	POLICY
001s	00067-a
001x	01902
003f	00013
005d	00013
005e	00036-c
005g	00145-f
.....	....
.....	....

POLICY-CLAIMS XREF

POLICY	CLAIM
00001-a	098s
00003	010d
00003-g	108h
00003-h	198d
00003-j	082j
00007	009s
....	.....
....	.....

The content of the two cross-reference tables is exactly the same, only the order is different. If it is desired to go from claims to policy, the claims/policy cross-reference table is used. And if it is desired to go from policy to claims, the policy/claims cross-reference table is used.

Another way to implement the relationship is to build a single cross-reference table and index the table twice, once on claims/policy and then again on policy/claims. Depending on how the application is to be used, this implementation or the one previously discussed, where two separate cross-reference tables are built, will be optimal.

Note that the relationships of data are completely divorced from the data in the base table. Were it not for the cross-reference tables, there would be no relationship between policies and claims whatsoever.

Recursive Relationship

A third type of relationship (discussed in later chapters) is the recursive relationship. A recursive relationship is one in which the relationship is not between two tables, but between data in the same table. Recursive relationships are common, occurring in the manufacturing bill of material, the organizational chart, and the common family tree.

A recursive relationship is classically built the same way that an m:n relationship is built, that is, using one or more cross-reference tables. The following example, based on the family tree, illustrates how two tables might be built to establish a recursive relationship.

PERSON TABLE

SSNO	NAME	HT	WT	SEX	DOB
459-70-1872	Inmon, W H	5'10"	210	M	07/20/45
321-00-1245	Nicks, Stevie	5'4"	120	F	08/11/52
450-12-6698	Slick, Grace	5'6"	115	F	06/05/44
776-12-9982	George, Boy	5'8"	135	M	07/02/56
778-09-7761	Estefan, Glor	5'2"	105	F	09/12/67
....	....	....	...	.	....
....	....	....	...	.	....

RELATIONSHIP TABLE

PARENT	CHILD
002-12-7786	009-12-7762
002-12-8977	981-00-2234
002-14-9822	998-23-9983
002-18-0988	334-55-3245
....	....
....	....

The two tables can be used to define the family tree relationship. Suppose it was desired to know how many children Roy Clark had. First the programmer finds Roy Clark's row in the PERSON table. From that row the SSNO of Roy is determined to be 445-89-7789.

Next the programmer looks up, in the RELATIONSHIP table, the entries for 445-89-7789. There are three entries in the relationship table for that SSNO. The three entries are:

```
445-89-7789  234-88-1002
445-89-7789  209-12-0092
445-89-7789  210-55-9073
```

The programmer then uses the value 234-88-1022 to go into the PERSON table to find out that Roy Clark has a son named Jackson. Similar entries into the PERSON table show that Roy's three children are named Jackson, Mark, and Mary. The ORACLE clause 'CONNECT BY' can be used to do the recursive processing automatically.

OPERATIONAL/DECISION SUPPORT ENVIRONMENTS

While not a part of ORACLE design, the application developer should understand the difference between the operational and the decision support (dss) environment. (For an in-depth discussion of the larger architecture of which operational and decision support processing are a part, refer to *Data Architecture: The Information Paradigm*, QED, 1989, and *Information Engineering For The Practitioner*, Yourdon Press, 1988.)

In the mature information processing environment, there are two separate environments: the operational environment and the decision support environment. The two environments are closely related to each other, but are physically separated. There are many reasons for the need to separate them:

OPERATIONAL	DECISION SUPPORT
▪ Repetitive processing	▪ Heuristic processing
▪ Detailed data	▪ Summarized data
▪ Transaction oriented	▪ Sequentially oriented
▪ Used clerically	▪ Used managerially
▪ High degree of structure of processing	▪ Hardly any structure in processing
▪ Quick response time	▪ Relaxed response time
▪ Data treated in its entirety	▪ Subsets of data processed

There are many more fundamental differences between operational and decision support processing, to the point that as organizations grow and the amount of processing done in both environments grows, there is a need for a formal separation of the two environments. The application designer should be aware of this need as the application is built.

SOME ORACLE TERMINOLOGY/ COMPONENTS

An "instance" of ORACLE refers to a hardware environment where ORACLE is up and running. For example, if one copy of ORACLE is running on a DEC VAX complex of processors, then that instance may be named instance A. And if another copy of ORACLE is running on an IBM mainframe as a started task and receiving transactions from CICS, that instance of ORACLE may be called instance B.

Another term the application needs to be aware of is an ORACLE "view." A view is simply a subset of a table. The view allows the subset to be accessed with no knowledge of other rows or columns residing in the table.

SUMMARY

In summary, in this section some basic concepts have been discussed. Keys have been introduced, along with several options such as concatenation and uniqueness. Clustering of data enhances performance where two or more tables are commonly accessed together based on common values. The batch window and the online transaction processing windows are separate and need to remain that way.

Certain utilities need to be designed as part of the application—recovery, reorganization, and loading and monitoring of data. In most cases the utilities supplied come with ORACLE; in some cases the utilities must be written by the programmer.

Finally data relationships were identified. Three common types of relationships that the application designer often runs into are the 1:n relationship, the m:n relationship with cross-reference tables, and the recursive relationship.

QUESTIONS: ORACLE—MORE BASICS

1. A key is a formal part of the ORACLE structuring of data. (T/F)

2. There are two types of keys: ______________ and ______________ keys.

3. A key may be ______________ or non ______________.

4. A key in ORACLE is supported by an ______________.
5. A key may be in a single column or on a ______________ column.
6. Only one type of data can be specified in a cluster. (T/F)
7. Data is clustered along ______________ key values.
8. Accessing clustered data is ______________ efficient.
9. Tables can be clustered:
   a. not at all
   b. once
   c. twice
   d. many times
10. Maintaining the physical location of data requires considerable resources at the point of:
    a. update
    b. deletion
    c. insertion
    d. access
11. Some options that ORACLE has to enhance the data management of clustered data are ______________ and ______________.
12. At the heart of performance is the physical activity of ______________.
13. I/O operates at ______________ speeds.
14. I/O is about ______________ to ______________ orders of magnitude slower than computer speeds.
15. There are two kinds of I/O, ______________ and ______________.
16. All types of I/O are slow. (T/F)
17. The designer SHOULD/SHOULD *not* depend on a large amount of virtual I/O to be done.
18. The typical processing day has two parts: ______________ and ______________.
19. The type of processing found in online processing is ______________.
20. The type of processing not found in online processing is ______________.
21. The type of processing found in the batch window is ______________.

22. Other programs typically found in the batch window are ______________.

23. The batch window typically is from the hours of ______________ to ______________.

24. Some types of utilities are ______________, ______________, ______________, ______________

25. ORACLE provides ALL/SOME/NONE of the utilities.

26. Name three types of relationships: ______________ , ______________, ______________.

27. A 1:n relationship typically entails the usage of a ______________.

28. One way to implement an m:n relationship is as two ______________ relationships.

29. But two 1:n relationships may cause ______________.

30. Another way to implement an m:n relationship is through building ______________ tables.

31. A recursive relationship occurs when a table has a relationship with ______________.

32. A recursive relationship is built the same way as an m:n relationship, using ______________.

33. The generic types of processing done can be classified as ______________ and ______________.

34. The two types of environments CANNOT/SHOULD/SHOULD NOT/UNDER MOST CIRCUMSTANCES SHOULD NOT be mixed.

35. Name some of the fundamental differences between operational and dss processing.

36. An "instance" is ______________.

37. A "view" is ______________.

38. A "view" MAY/MAY NOT be over more than one table.

39. For performance reasons, a view SHOULD NOT/SHOULD be over more than one table.

CHAPTER 3

Conceptual Data Base Design—Normalization

(Note: for a detailed discussion of the topics that are discussed in this chapter, refer to *Information Engineering for the Practitioner*, Yourdon Press, 1988 and to *Data Architecture: The Information Paradigm*, QED, 1989.)

There are two steps to data base design: conceptual data base design and physical data base design. The remaining chapters in this book address various aspects of physical data base and transaction design. This chapter is on conceptual data base design.

Conceptual (or logical) data base design forms the basis of physical data base design. In one form or the other the data, the structure of data, and the relationships of data must be established before the activities of physical data base design can commence. And there are many ways to collect and assimilate those pieces of information required of the conceptual model of data. Some of the ways are:

- Formal data analysis—normalization of data
- Data architecture—information system architecture
- In-house techniques developed over the years

The starting point for most data base applications should be the corporate data model (assuming the corporation has a data model!) Most mature corporations have built and maintain what can be termed the corporate data model, which is a collection of the global information needs of the enterprise. Generally speaking, the corporate data model identifies the major pieces of data and the major relationships that are required. In addition, the corporate data model identifies which of those components are already in existence.

THE CORPORATE DATA MODEL

The application designer needs to become acquainted with the corporate data model for a variety of reasons:

- To identify what design work has already been done.
- To identify what systems have already been built to see if there is an opportunity to build on existing systems rather than having to build everything from scratch.
- To identify what future requirements must be factored into the design to pave the way for future efforts.

The second activity the application designer must undertake is to separate the data elements that have been identified into two classifications: primitive data and derived data. In all but the most unusual of systems, it is a mistake to freely mix the two types of data, especially at the point of conceptual data base design. In every case, the conceptual data model centers around primitive data. IT IS A MISTAKE TO TRY TO MODEL DERIVED DATA!!

The data that is collected may come from a variety of sources, including existing reports, screens, reports, etc. Other sources include end user interviews, a review of past modeling efforts, a statement of requirements, and so forth. The sources of data are as abundant as the imagination of the application designer.

As data requirements are gathered, so too are processing requirements. However, processing requirements are handled quite differently from data requirements.

LEVELS OF MODELING

Generally speaking, the data model for the application (as far as conceptual design is concerned) has two levels—a high level and a mid-level. The high level (sometimes called the subject level, or the ERD level) consists of the major components of the application and their relationships to each other. This level of data model is devoid of detail and serves to identify the major subjects the application will center on.

The mid-level of modeling is where the detail of the model is collected. Each major subject of the high-level model has its own unique mid-level model that reflects its data requirements.

Analogically, the high-level model is equivalent to a model of the earth—a globe—while the mid-level model is equivalent to a map of Texas.

As a simple example of a high-level model, a bank may construct the model shown:

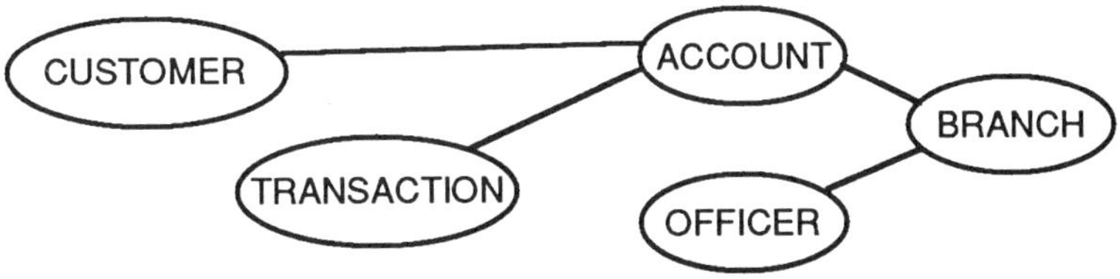

A simple example of a mid-level data model for the bank might be for transaction, as shown:

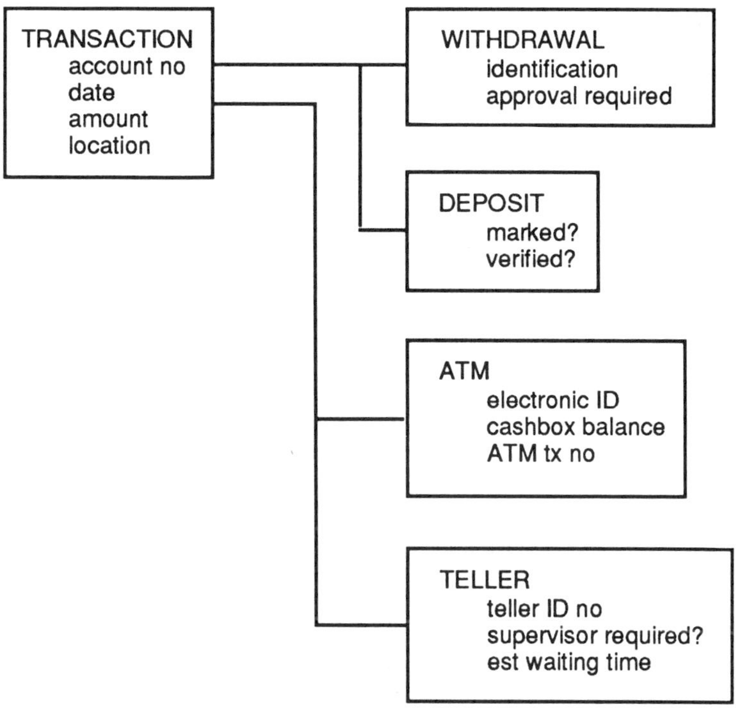

The mid-level model shows that there is generic information about a transaction such as the account the transaction went against, the date of the transaction, and so forth. All transactions have this information common to them. There are different types of transactions as well. One type is a withdrawal. Information peculiar to a withdrawal includes identification required by the teller and whether approval was required.

Unique information about a deposit includes whether the depositor asked for the deposit to be marked and whether the source of funds was verified.

Another type of information about a transaction is the delivery mechanism used to execute the transaction. This category includes ATM activity and teller activity. Information peculiar to ATM or teller processing is included in this group of information.

Given that there are two types of categories represented in this simple data model, the model would apply to ATM withdrawals, ATM deposits, teller withdrawals, and teller deposits.

OUTPUT FROM THE MID-LEVEL MODEL

The basic output of the mid-level model—that serving as input into the physical model—includes:

- The identification of the primitive data elements
- The grouping of the data elements
- The relationships between the groups of data elements
- The primary keys of the groupings of data elements
- The secondary keys of the data elements

The primitive data elements come from the many sources previously mentioned. The data elements are combined according to their "existence dependency criteria." "Existence dependency criteria" is a sophisticated name for an activity familiar to every experienced data designer. It means that data should be grouped with other data elements whose existence depends directly and entirely on the same key.

For example, suppose the primary key of a group of data elements was the social security number of a person. Then the name of the person depends directly on the social security number. Once you know the social security number of the person, you know his or her name. And the direct personal descriptors of the person, such as date of birth, height, weight, and sex, apply directly to the social security number as well. If it is known that social security number 459-70-1872 belongs to W. H. Inmon, then the name, age, sex, and so forth, can be directly discovered. Therefore, the data elements name, date of birth, height, weight, and sex share the same existence dependency criteria and in fact should be grouped together in the data model.

But what about the work phone number of an individual? Does it share the same existence dependency criteria as other data elements such as name and height? It in fact does not share the same existence dependency criteria. While there may be a relationship between a given social security number and a phone number at a point in time, it is not the same relationship at all. For example, there may be many people sharing the same phone number, but more important, the phone number does not depend on any given social security number for its existence. If a person dies, then the directly dependent data elements lose relevance. But if a person dies, a telephone number remains with no loss of relevance. Therefore, a work telephone number should not be grouped with name, date of birth, and sex. The result of the structuring of data according to existence dependency criteria is the normalization of data.

Another feature of the data model is the ability to identify types of data. As seen in the example, a transaction had both common data and data elements that applied to only one type of the data. And there were different categories for typing the data. One category of transactions was withdrawals/deposits. Another type was ATM/teller transactions.

After the groups of data elements are created, the relationship between them must be created. Based on the business usage of the data, relationships are identified. There are (at least!) two kinds of relationships: relationships between a group of data and its subtypes and relationships between groups of data based on the high-level model. The relationship of groups of data to their subtypes has already been discussed.

The relationship between groups of data based on the major business relationships stems directly from the high-level data model. At the high level of data modeling, major subjects and their relationships have been identified. For example, in the high-level data model that was shown, the major subject account had relationships with customers, branches, transactions, and other customers.

These relationships are depicted in the mid-level data model as a connector or foreign key between groups of data.

Each group of data has its own unique key. (In some circumstances

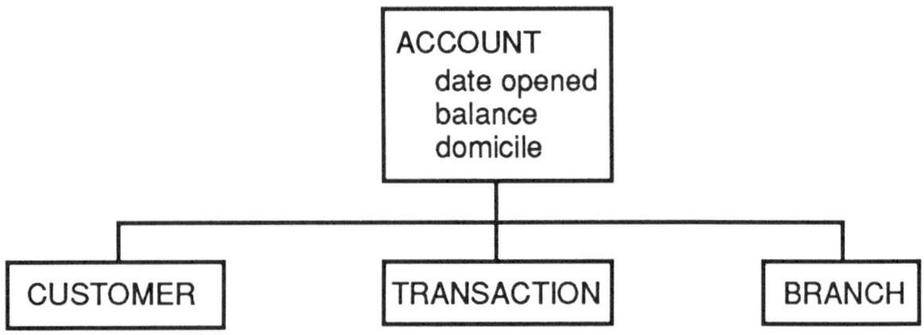

the key may not actually be unique, but in most circumstances it is.) The key serves as the basis for determining the existence dependency criteria of the group of data. The key is called the "primary key" and is usually the field that becomes indexed at the point of physical design. If the group of data becomes clustered, the primary key is the most likely candidate for clustering.

There may be other keys in a group of data. These are called "secondary keys" and may or may not have an index attached to them at the point of physical design.

The mid-level data model contains no redundant data at the end of the modeling exercise (foreign keys excepted). Every nonkey data element fits in one and only one grouping of data at the end of the mid-level modeling exercise.

THE CORPORATE MODEL AND THE MID-LEVEL MODEL

An activity the designer should undertake before the mid-level model can be declared finished is to compare the mid-level model to the corporate data model. Any discrepancies in content and structure should be reconciled. Either the corporate data model needs to be changed or the application data model needs to be changed.

Another useful activity at this point is to gather the volumes of data, by grouping of data, and the frequency of access. The volume and frequency are needed for the first physical data base design activity, which is the denormalization of data.

In addition to the frequencies of execution and the volumes of data, the application designer needs to consider encoding structures at the time. For the data found in the groupings of data, what encoding will be done, and will the encoding be done uniformly across all users of the application? The issue of encoding is especially important for rewrites of applications or large maintenance activities where the resulting system will replace one or more systems already in existence.

THE DATA MODEL AND DERIVED DATA

The data model reflects (and properly so!) only the primitive data of the enterprise. But derived data is not a second-class citizen. Where does derived data fit in the grand scheme of things? It fits in the dss environment, almost exclusively. It is easier to build systems with derived data than it is to model them. Derived systems typically grow faster than they can be modeled. As long as the primitive basis for the derived data is reflected in the data model, then there is no need to put derived data in the data model.

At the same time that the data model is being built, there are other corresponding activities occurring for process modeling. In some cases, the process modeling activities occurring independently are:

- Functional decomposition
- Data flow diagramming
- Mini spec preparation, and
- A variety of other activities.

When the data model (i.e., the mid-level data model) is complete, it should be compared to the process model (which hopefully will be complete or at least comprehensible at this point in time.) The application designer should insure that:

- All data in the data model is supported in the process model. The data should have specifications for insertion, deletion, update, and access in the process model.
- All data referenced in the process model should be able to be found in the data model. If the process model begins to reference data elements that are not in the data model or that are not able to be derived from data in the data model, then there is a discrepancy between the two models.

At the end of the data collection, the data assimilation, design, and other review activities, the following should be the output of the conceptual data base design step:

- The primitive data elements of the application.
- The grouping of the data elements.
- The primary and secondary keys of the groupings of data.
- An identification of the relationships between the different groupings of data.

Once the application designer has completed all these activities and produced the appropriate output, the design is ready to go into physical data base design.

SUMMARY

This first step to building successful applications is to understand the data on which the applications run. This is done through the building of a data model. The data model has three levels—a high level, a mid-level, and a low level. While the data model is built for an application, it is necessary to compare and contrast the application data model to the corporate data model.

QUESTIONS: CONCEPTUAL DATA BASE DESIGN—NORMALIZATION

1. There are, generically, two kinds of data base design: ______________ and ______________.
2. ______________ is done before physical data base design.
3. There ARE MANY/IS ONLY ONE way(s) to do conceptual data base design.
4. One of the central components of conceptual data base design is the ______________ model.
5. In addition to the data model, usually a ______________ is created as well.
6. There usually is a ______________ data model.
7. The application needs to be aware of what the corporate data looks like and what the differences between the application model and the corporate data model are. (T/F)
8. The application model IS ALWAYS/IS SOMETIMES/OUGHT TO BE a subset of the corporate data model.
9. There are two broad classifications of data: ______________ and ______________.

10. It is a mistake to try to model derived data. (T/F)

11. The conceptual data model is made up almost entirely of ______________ data.

12. The source of data for the conceptual data model comes from (name three): ______________, ______________, and ______________.

13. The conceptual model is made up of two levels of modeling: ______________ and ______________.

14. The high level of modeling is often called the ______________.

15. The mid-level model contains (name four): ______________, ______________, ______________, and ______________.

16. Data is grouped according to ______________.

17. Relationships identified at the high-level model DO/DO NOT appear at the mid-level.

18. No redundancy of data is found at the mid-level. (T/F)

19. Other useful information collected with the mid-level model includes:

20. Derived data IS/IS NOT directly represented in the conceptual data model.

21. Derived data IS/IS NOT indirectly represented in the conceptual data model.

22. Name some process model activities.

CHAPTER 4

Conceptual Data Base Design—Denormalization

The performance of relational systems can be enhanced through the physical placement of data in an optimal fashion. The result of normalization is usually many small tables of data. When data must be dynamically joined, the result is the consumption of much I/O. There may be significant performance gains to be made by "denormalizing" the data, immediately prior to physical data base design.

In every case, normalization of data is encouraged as a basis for the logical design of data. But when it comes time to translate the logical design into a physical design, the practice of selectively denormalizing data according to the organization's usage of data is advocated.

Denormalization, then, is the design process of taking normalized data and producing a physical design in which normalized data is rearranged so that optimal access and manipulation of data can be achieved. Denormalizing data usually means consolidating data into larger groups of data than that specified by the normalized structure. But in some cases, as discussed later, denormalizing data requires that data be split into even smaller groups of data than that specified by normalization.

A good example of physical denormalization of data in ORACLE is clustering of data. When data is clustered, different types of data can be physically colocated based on a common kcy value. The data remains normalized at the logical level and denormalized at the physical level.

NORMALIZATION OF DATA

The process of normalization (which is one of the foundations of relational technology) requires that data be organized into individual tables. Each table is distinct from other tables and has its own unique key. All of the nonkey data in a table logically depends on the full key of the table for its existence. For example, in a table representing an employee, the key of the employee may be employee number, and the nonkey information may include date of hire, location of hire, starting position, and so forth. If an employee did not exist there would be no date of hire or location of hire. The nonkey data depends on the key data for its existence. Figure 1 shows a simple normalized table.

Prior to physical data base design, all data is normalized into relational tables. One result of normalization is that the tables defined tend to have few data elements in each table, and there tends to be many tables. There is nothing inherently wrong with this very fine division of data, but if a high volume of processing is to be done and if the processing requires frequent reference from one table to the next, then the result is the consumption of much I/O. And when much

EMPLOYEE NUMBER	DATE HIRE	LOCATION	CONDITIONS
0012	850312	Tuscon, AZ	finish degree
0015	701215	El Paso, TX	--------------------
0018	750730	Tempe, AZ	--------------------
0020	761116	Dallas, TX	--------------------
0022	771215	Houston, TX	no part time work
0024	821217	Waco, TX	complete CPA
0025	791010	Pecos, TX	--------------------
0028	810801	Las Cruces, NM	--------------------
--------	-----------	-----------------	--------------------

FIGURE 1. A simple normalized table—each nonkey column depends on the key for its existence.

I/O is consumed the result is poor performance. Figure 2 illustrates the dynamic joining of several relational tables.

Note that if the high-volume processing goes against only data in a single table, then the techniques of denormalization do not apply. When high-performance processing goes against a single table, then combining tables (i.e., denormalizing tables) has little or no effect on performance and the I/O consumed. It is only when processing frequently must jump from one table to the next that denormalization will enhance performance. Denormalization will also enhance performance of the offline environment if there is a heavy amount of processing occurring in batch and if the batch processing frequently jumps from one table to the next.

Thus, denormalization, in most cases, is the process of taking many small tables and combining them into fewer, larger tables, so that less I/O is required. Figure 3 shows a table that has been denormalized.

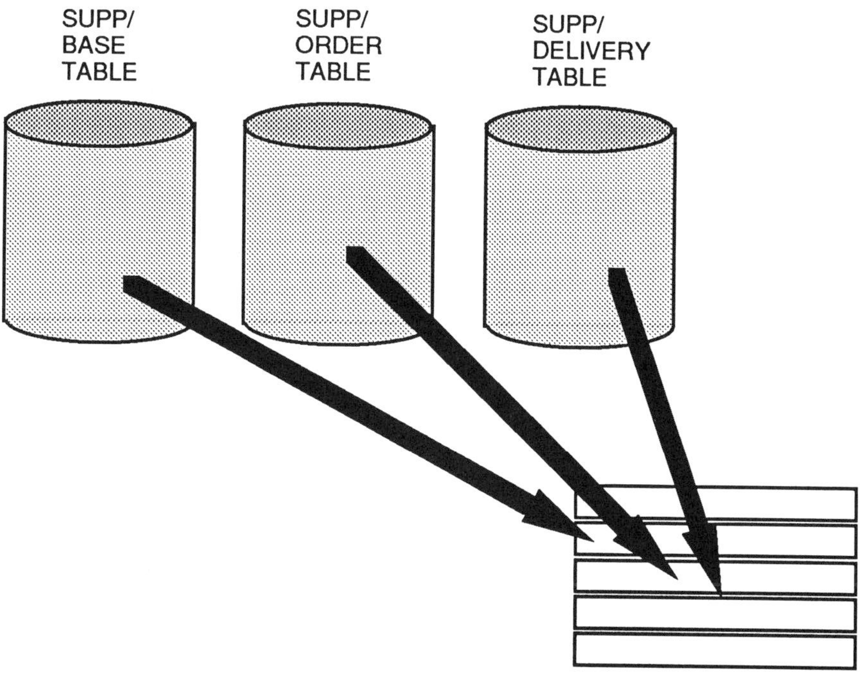

FIGURE 2. The dynamic joining of several relational tables.

EMP NO	NAME	ADDRESS	AGE	MANAGER	PHONE	SCHOOL
0013	G Frey	123 Main St	39	N Diamond	667-0097	Yale
0016	D Henley	1689 1st	45	E John	556-0094	Harvard
0019	T Schmitt	134 Grand	43	N Sedaka	009-6675	Clemson
0021	J Walsh	930 Teton	42	C King	556-0096	Georgia
0201	D Felder	1455 Tincup	41	J P Carson	778-9904	Princeton
0202	B Leadon	220 Pine	43	E McMahon	776-9904	Cal Tech
0204	S Nicks	220 Pine	39	Dr Severinson	776-0094	Stanford
-------	----------	------------	---	------------	---------	-----------

FIGURE 3. An unnormalized table.

The data elements in the same row in Figure 3 have different existence criteria and as such are not normalized.

THE USAGE MATRIX

The first step in the denormalization of data is to determine what processes represent the heaviest volume and what tables those processes are operating on. A convenient aid in this analysis is to create a matrix, matching process against table. Going down the left-hand side of the matrix are the tables that are being analyzed. Going across the page are the processes that are being analyzed. Figure 4 shows an example of a usage matrix.

Each cell in the matrix, then, represents the access of the table by the process.

After the matrix is created, the first (rather raw) analysis is to determine how many times the process will be executed, usually for a 24-hour period. (Note: Some period of time must be chosen as a baseline for the building of the table/process matrix.) Then the number of times the process will operate against the table is calculated for every table. For example, if process A accesses tables 2, 5, and 6, and if process A executes 100 times a day, then the cell representing the intersection of process A and tables 2, 5, and 6 will contain the value

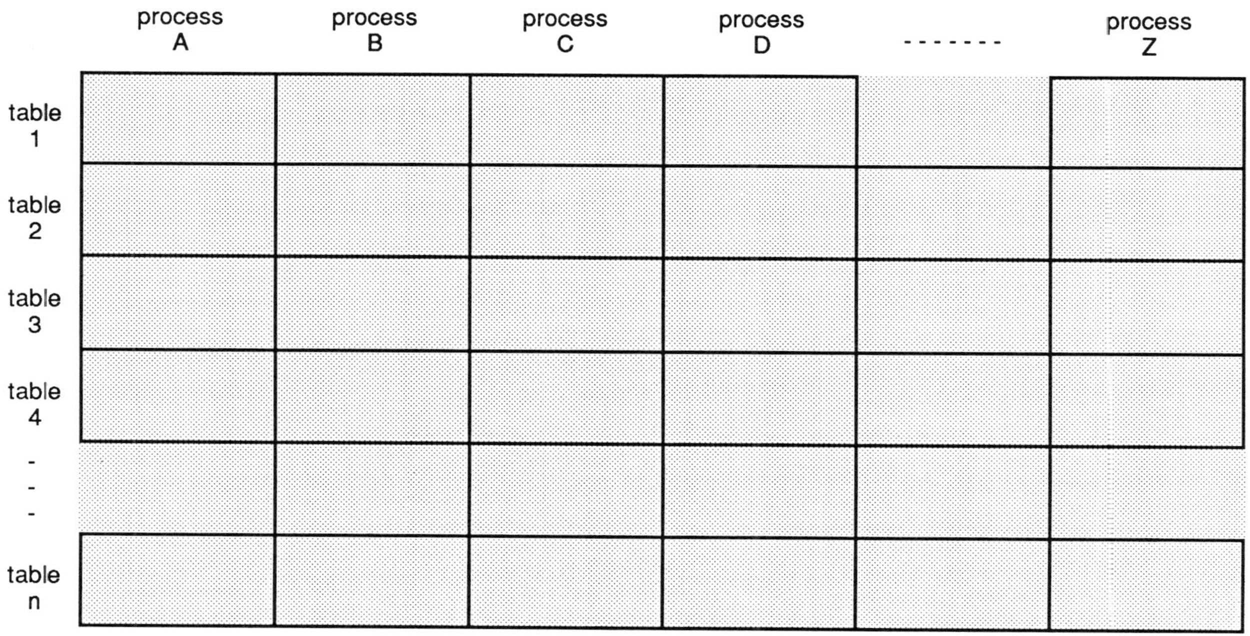

FIGURE 4. The process/table usage matrix.

100, and other cells where the table was not accessed will contain a value of zero.

In addition to merely accessing data, the analyst may wish to use the usage matrix to keep track of update and access information. In other words, it may be useful to distinguish between access and update for some types of processes.

The estimate of the number of executions for a process can become complex because of several factors. In some cases, a process has never been run before and the number of times the process will be executed is purely a guess. In other cases, the process will execute 100 times on one day and 1000 times on another day, in a random pattern. And in still other cases, a process will require high performance while another will not need the same level of performance. Still another factor is that a transaction will show an execution frequency of 1000 and a batch process will show a frequency of execution of 1 or 2 for the same 24-hour period.

THE PROCESSING FREQUENCY ANOMALIES

All of these anomalies need to be taken into account if the denormalization process is to be effective. In the case where the number of times a process is to execute is not known, generally speaking the highest reasonable estimate should be used. The estimate may come from empirically derived data or it may be analytically derived. In any case, to err slightly too high is acceptable; to err too low is not acceptable.

In the case where there is a substantial difference between one day's processing activities and another day's activities, the high-water mark should be used.

In the case where there is a substantial difference between the priorities of different transactions, the transactions with the higher priorities should be weighted in favor of the more important transactions. The weighting is done by multiplying the number of transactions run per day by a factor of 2 or 3.

All differences have been accounted for with the exception of that between batch and online processing. For example, the frequency of execution of an online process may be 400 times a day, while the frequency of execution of a batch process may be 2 times a day.

ESTIMATING ROW ACCESS FREQUENCY

After the number of executions has been placed in the appropriate cell in the matrix, the next step is to determine how many rows of the table will be needed by each execution. In other words, when a process accesses a table, how many rows will it normally access.

For example, the value in one cell may be 150, indicating that a process will access a table 150 times throughout the day. The next cell has a value of 200. The analysis now requires that the number of accesses be multiplied by the number of rows per access. The first process accesses one row per access, and the next process accesses 25 rows per access. Factoring in the number of rows per execution leaves values of 150 and 5000 in the two cells. The values in the cells are now more representative of the true processing needs of the system.

The number of accesses per execution is in some cases a very straightforward number and in other cases is not. For example, suppose a process accesses 5 and only 5 rows per execution, then it is clear that the process frequency for the cell needs to be multiplied by 5. For another cell suppose that the average number of rows accessed is 10, with a standard deviation of .5. This means that most executions will use 10 rows. The cell is multiplied by 10. But suppose the average number of rows accessed per execution is 15, with a standard deviation of 12.5. In this case there is a wide variance between the number of rows accessed per execution. As a rule, one half of the standard deviation should be added to the mean as the factor to be applied to the frequency of execution. In the example being discussed, one half of 12.5 is 6.25, which is added to 15, yielding 21.25, which is the factor that should be used.

At this point, batch processing is factored in. A batch process may show only one execution per day, but in executing, the batch process accesses 40,000 rows.

Another possibility for the usage of the matrix is the balancing of large tables versus small tables. A large table may be assumed to enjoy fewer buffer hits, while a smaller table may enjoy more buffer hits. The tables may be weighted accordingly, by assigning a weight of 2 or 3 to the larger tables.

HEURISTIC AND ITERATIVE ANALYSIS

The next analytical step is to determine two things—which tables should be combined and which tables should be clustered. The analysis to follow is heuristic and iterative, and does not follow any prescriptive path.

The first pass at denormalization is to attempt to combine the most heavily used tables. The total row/table usage may be calculated from the table by adding each line to the right. In other words, the total number of rows needed for all processing is the sum of all row accesses going across the page. Based upon the total numbers of usage, the analyst asks the question: Which two or more rows can be merged so that data used together is placed in the same row?

Generally speaking, the rows that can be combined share part of a common key. For example, an employee base table, an employee education table, and an employee job history table may be able to be combined. But an employee and a parts usage table would not be candidates for tables that could be combined. The first cut at analysis is to identify heavily used tables that are logical candidates for combination. Key commonality is the first clue to the successful combination of data.

However, not all commonly shared keys can be successfully combined. Consider the simple case of a bank balance table and a bank activity table, where activities add up to the current balance. Certainly these tables share a common key and certainly they are used together, but the distribution of keys is so dissimilar that the pieces of data are combined only with difficulty. For example, activity may be incorporated into the balance table, but activity is frequently updated and occurs a variable number of times. Figure 5 illustrates the difficulties of combining balance and activity rows.

Admittedly some savings can be effected, but at a cost of complexity, which is most likely undesirable.

After the candidates that can be merged together are merged, then the savings analysis is done. In the perfect case, table A is accessed 1000 times and table B is accessed 5000 times per day. By combining the tables, all accesses to B will be combined with accesses to A. The total number of accesses to the combined A/B is 1000 in the optimal case.

The advantage of the usage matrix is that it allows different combinations of data to be merged and allows the different economies of consolidation to be measured quantitatively.

Of course, the analyst should carefully consider the full range of design criteria when combining two tables. Such issues as the ability to split the data at a later point in time or the creation of very large tables should be considered along with the performance considerations.

ACCT	BALANCE	ACTIVITY	DATE
10089	100.00	+25.00	1215
10089	75.00	-25.00	1216
10089	150.00	+50.00	1216
10089	189.36	+39.36	1217
10089	60.36	-120.00	1218
10089	1060.36	+1000.00	1218
-------	-----------	----------	-------

The table that results when balance is superimposed on activity. A new balance is created every time there is an activity, and there is much duplication of key data.

		ACTIVITY 1		ACTIVITY 2			ACTIVITY n	
ACCT	BAL	DATE	AMT	DATE	AMT	------------	DATE	AMT
10089	1060.36	1215	+25.00	1216	-25.00	-----------	1218	+1000.00
10091	1078.98	1218	-1000.00	1219	+35.00	-----------	-------	------------
10092	10908.00	1215	+15000.00	1221	-10.00	-----------	1221	+12000.00
10092.1	------------	1222	-12000.00	1224	+2798.76	-----------	1224	+35997.00
10094	------------	-------	------------	-------	---------	-----------	-------	-----------
--------	------------	-------	------------	-------	---------	-----------	-------	-----------

The table that results when activity is superimposed on balance. There are a widely varying number of activities for each account for the same period of time. Some accounts have no activity – such as account 10094 and other accounts have so much activity that more than one row must be used. When more than one row is used – as in the case of account 10092, the application convention is that the active balance is stored in the first occurrence of the account.

FIGURE 5. The difficulties of combining balance and activity rows.

CLUSTERING ANALYSIS

Considered in combination with the consolidation of tables is the issue of whether data should be clustered or not. When the total number of table accesses was calculated, no consideration was given to the physical access of data. A single physical access is one where only a single row is accessed. A multiple access is one where one row after another is accessed in rapid succession based on a common key value. When data is clustered and much multiple access occurs, then it may be assumed that multiple rows may be read in a single I/O (i.e., as many rows as exist in a block). In the analysis of which rows need to be combined, the issue of clustering can be factored in. When it is assumed that rows are clustered the total number of physical accesses is adjusted in the matrix to reflect the lessened need for I/O.

A further refinement in the access of clustered data is whether the access of data will be for the purposes of reading or updating. If access is for the purpose of updating, it is assumed that there will be minimal locking of data. However, if there is update that can occur, then it must be assumed that data locking will be a factor.

AUTOMATED TOOLS

The optimal plan for denormalization and clustering of data is the combination of consolidation of data and clustering that reduces the TOTAL number of accesses to the data in the system. Because of the number of tables and because of the combinations that are possible, this phase of denormalization analysis is heuristic and iterative. It often makes sense to use a spreadsheet tool such as LOTUS 1-2-3 as an aid in this phase of analysis. In using an automated tool, not only can different options be documented, but new options can be calculated rapidly.

As an example of a successful table denormalization, suppose a supplier/order table and an order/supplier line item table have been specified by the data analysis and normalization process. The supplier/order table contains information about who the supplier of an order is, the supplier contact, and name and phone number, as well as conditions of the order. The order/supplier line item table contains information about the line items of an order, the amount of each item ordered, the price, and so forth. Most processes that access one table access the other. Creating a single table allows access to be done in a single I/O, since consolidation forces the data into the same row. Figure 6 shows the effect of consolidation.

					ITEM 1		
SUPP	ORD	CONTACT	PHONE	COND	PART	AMT	PRICE
10098	67-009	P McCartney	555-8907	FOB	110-a	9000	100.00
10100	8-165	R Starr	899-7765	COD	1187	1	6000.00
10100	978-1	G Harrison	667-0098	-----	1187	1	5500.00
10100	7-009	J Lennon	445-6679	FOB	22098	20	998.45
10102	5-890	M Jagger	978-1659	FOB	110-s	20	776.00
10103	445-6	H Nillson	887-0092	COD	1187	1	16000.00
----------	-------	----------	----------	-----	-------	----	------------

	ITEM n			ITEM n + 1	
PART	AMT	PRICE	PART	AMT	PRICE
1998	5	556.00	--------	------	----------
------	-------	--------	--------	------	----------
390-p	400	56.09	445rtp	56	998.02
343	2	450.00	---------	------	---------
546-y	5600	23.09	45-rty	5600	899.00
567u-o	3	45099.98	---------	------	----------
------	-------	--------	---------	------	---------

FIGURE 6. The consolidation of two tables into a denormalized table.

REDUNDANCY

After the analysis is done, another variable has to be considered—the deliberate introduction of redundancy into the system. To this point it has been assumed that the data in the system was nonredundant. The nonredundancy of data optimizes update of data at the expense of access of data. The issue of denormalization now must address the question, Will the deliberate introduction of redundancy into the system significantly reduce the total amount of accesses that the system makes?

This analysis is addressed heuristically and iteratively, as was the previous analysis. The first clue as to which data elements are candidates for redundant existence comes from the frequency matrix that has been developed. Those tables that are being frequently accessed and not frequently updated may contain data that, when positioned redundantly in more than one table, reduces total access needs. Of course, the analyst must keep in mind that the proliferation of data may reduce access needs but increases update needs when the data values change. Generally speaking, only limited amounts of data are deliberately proliferated.

As an example of the selective use of redundancy, suppose there is a parts table, a supplier table, and a cross reference table. The cross reference table contains only the key values: part and supplier. It is found that when the cross reference table is used in going from part to supplier, in most cases only the supplier name and address are needed. Other information contained in the supplier table is accessed only infrequently. The analyst places supplier name and address in the parts/supplier cross reference table as nonkey data as shown in Figure 7.

Supplier name and address are not placed in the supplier/parts cross reference table. Now, when cross reference needs to be made to the supplier, only the part/supplier cross reference table must be accessed, saving an access to the supplier table. The analyst must factor into the savings the work required by the system to keep the supplier name and address current in the cross reference table. The cross reference table must be updated—potentially in many places—when supplier name and address change. Fortunately, the fields that have been made redundant are stable fields and do not require frequent maintenance.

After the redundancy analysis is done, the analyst adjusts the matrix to reflect the new pattern of access and update of tables.

PART	SUPP	SUPP NAME	SUPP ADDRESS
1009	10098	Emporium	123 Grand
1009	10198	Grand Auto	17th Street
1009	19087	Wilson Hdwre	16 N Ranch Rd
1009	20098	Emporium	123 Grand
1010	10098	Denver Dry	16th St Mall
1011	1099	Denver Dry	16th St Mall
-------	----------	--------------	--------------

FIGURE 7. A cross-reference table with supplier name and address added.

INTERNAL ARRAYS

Another technique of denormalization available to the analyst is the specification of internal arrays of data in a row. If a row contains a small number of nonkey data elements, if the data elements are frequently accessed in a sequential manner, if the pattern of access is stable, and if the number of occurrences of nonkey data can be reliably calculated for the key values of a table, then the analyst should consider violating the first form of normalization by placing the elements of data into an array. In an array, a row contains multiple occurrences of nonkey data. When the conditions are met, a substantial savings in resources consumed is possible.

As an example of the usage of an array within a row, consider a payroll history file. The logical design specifies that the twice-monthly paycheck be stored individually. But there is no reason why an annual payroll history table cannot be created. The annual table contains 24 occurrences—one for each twice-monthly paycheck. The order of insertion of the occurrences of data, the number of occurrences for each employee, and the access of the occurrences are very stable. The violation of the first form of normalization yields many performance dividends, not to mention the savings of space in the reduced need for key data. Figure 8 shows this form of denormalization.

EMP NO	PAY 01/15	PAY 01/30	PAY 02/15	PAY 02/28	----------
0021	1500.00	1500.00	1500.00	1500.00	----------
0023	1789.00	1775.00	1789.00	1796.00	----------
0024	1050.50	1100.00	1050.89	1100.00	----------
0026	998.00	1025.90	1229.00	1356.00	----------
0029	767.00	760.98	785.90	786.45	----------
0031	1976.00	1234.00	1879.92	1876.34	----------
-------	----------	----------	----------	----------	----------

FIGURE 8. A pay history table with individual pay amounts organized into an array.

OTHER OPTIONS

The design techniques for denormalization to this point have merged data into the same row so that a minimum of I/O is used, once the row is accessed. But merging unlike data is not the only denormalization technique. Suppose a bank account table is to be created. The key of the table is the account, and nonkey elements include bank balance, domicile, date account opened and other similar elements. The key—account number—is 16 bytes in length and the nonkey data is 64 bytes in length. Total row space is 80 bytes.

To enhance performance, the table is split into two tables. One table contains the account key and balance. A row in this table is 22 bytes in length. The other table contains the key and all the other nonkey data elements—other than balance. The length of a row in this table is 74 bytes.

An analysis of the accounts table shows that the frequency of access of the balance data is heavy. Every time an activity against an account is transacted, the balance table is accessed and updated. The remaining account data—domicile, date account opened, etc.—is accessed very infrequently.

By splitting the data into separate tables, the probability of a fortuitous hit in the buffer is raised. In the original design, a row was 80 bytes in length. In a fully packed 4k buffer, about 50 rows will fit. In the new design, for the balance table about 180 rows will fit in the buffer. The odds of a fortuitous buffer hit are raised by shrinking the size of the row with the most activity and packing the highly accessed data together so that there is a greater chance of a buffer hit.

This technique of denormalization, then, is a radical departure from other techniques of denormalization that rely on the consolidation of data.

SUMMARY

In summary, this chapter has focused on what denormalization is and why it can enhance performance. The building of a usage matrix to determine the effectiveness of denormalization was discussed, as well as the heuristic and iterative analysis that centers around the matrix. It is suggested that an automated tool such as a spreadsheet be used to create and maintain the matrix. Finally, the deliberate introduction of redundancy into the system was suggested.

Some of the design techniques for denormalization include:

- Clustering data
- Creating arrays of data
- Creating redundancy selectively
- Consolidating tables of data
- Splitting data into smaller tables based on different patterns of utilization

QUESTIONS: CONCEPTUAL DATA BASE DESIGN—DENORMALIZATION

1. Normalization of data is one of the foundations of _______________ theory.
2. In a normalized table, each _______________ field depends on the _______________ field for its existence.
3. The result of normalization is that data is separated into MANY/FEW tables.
4. When data is separated into many tables and those tables are turned into physical data bases, data is widely _______________.
5. The dispersion of data costs I/O when those tables must be _______________ joined by an application program.
6. The performance implications of normalization APPLY/APPLY PRIMARILY/DO NOT APPLY to the batch environment.

7. The performance implications of normalization IMPLY/DO NOT IMPLY that normalization should not be done.
8. Denormalization is the process of arranging ____________ in other than its normalized form.
9. Usually denormalization requires that normalized tables be combined into a single ____________.
10. When data is combined into a single table, it can ALWAYS/USUALLY/SOMETIMES be accessed with a single I/O.
11. For data to be combined in a single table, a ____________ key is required.
12. Furthermore, for data to be combined in a single table, the ____________ frequency must be similar or the same.
13. Combining data into a single row has NO/SOME/A LARGE effect on performance unless many processes access all the data in a single execution.
14. The data that is denormalized should be sensitive to the frequency of execution of the processes. (T/F)
15. Another form of denormalization is the splitting of data into very small tables, which maximizes the probability of a fortuitous ____________ hit.
16. Concentrating on buffer hits is an issue only for HIGH/LOW performance data.
17. A usage matrix table suggests what rows should be combined and what rows should be indexed and/or ____________.
18. A row that is heavily used and accessed in a sequential manner is an ideal candidate for ____________.
19. A row can SOMETIMES/NEVER UNDER ANY CONDITIONS/EASILY be clustered more than once.
20. An application partitioned data base MUST/MAY BE clustered.
21. Another form of denormalization that may reduce the total accesses required is the deliberate introduction of ____________.
22. Redundancy maximizes access of data at the expense of ____________ of data.
23. Usually data that is VOLATILE/STABLE is a candidate for redundancy.
24. The designer may reduce the number of accesses required by the introduction of redundancy, but the designer must factor in the

accesses required to update the data when the data ________
________.

25. When multiple occurrences of data are placed in a single row, the ________ level of normalization is violated.
26. Arrays of data in a row can save I/O in that, in SOME/MOST/ALL rows, only one I/O will be needed to access all data in the array.
27. Whether to place data in an array in a row DEPENDS ON/DOES NOT DEPEND ON how often and in what pattern the data is to be used and updated.
28. Arrays of data in a row can also save SOME/MUCH space in that the repetition of keys is not necessary.
29. When data from two different tables is loaded into a page of a simple tablespace so that there is a relationship between the keys of the two tables, ________ of data has occurred.

CHAPTER 5

Physical Data Base Design in ORACLE

INDEXING DATA

One of the biggest performance considerations of ORACLE is the selection of columns for indexing. The issue of indexing columns has two facets: in accessing data, indexes can greatly reduce I/O requirements, but in the loading and update of data, indexes can cost I/O. The issue of creating, maintaining, and using indexes, then, is one of a tradeoff between the access of data and the update/loading of data.

To illustrate the potential I/O savings of an index, consider the simple relational table shown in Figure 9.

Figure 9 shows a table that contains an employee's educational history. Consider the I/O required to service the request to find all employees who attended Arizona University.

```
SELECT EMPLOYEE
FROM EMPTAB
WHERE SCHOOL = "ARIZ'
```

This request against an unindexed employee's data requires that all rows in all pages be queried. In short, if there are *n* pages, then *n* I/Os will be required to service the request.

But suppose the table in Figure 9 were indexed for each employee on school attended, as shown in Figure 10.

	EMP NO	DATE ATTENDED	SCHOOL	DEGREE	MAJOR
page 1	1456	1967	Yale	---	Math
	1456	1970	Arizona	BS	Math
	1456	1972	Arizona	MS	Comp Sci
	1459	1981	Miami	BS	Business
	--------	-------	----------	---	----------
page 2	1701	1968	UCLA	BS	Civil Eng
	1714	1979	Harvard	BS	English
	1714	1984	U Texas	MS	English
	1743	1980	U Colorado	---	Anthropology
	1752	1963	Dartmouth	BS	Spanish
	-------	-------	-----------	---	----------

FIGURE 9. An employee education table whose primary key is employee/date of attendance.

Figure Figure 10 shows that with the index (which is highly condensed into a few blocks of data), the query of which employees went to Arizona University is easily answered. The school-attended index is accessed, and, based upon the information found in the index, only those pages and rows that are appropriate are physically accessed. In short, instead of accessing all pages and randomly searching for data that fits the criteria, the index allows data to be precisely and directly accessed, thus greatly economizing on the I/Os required to satisfy a request.

But indexes can save I/O in other ways. Suppose the end user wished to see not the names of the employees that went to Arizona University but merely a count of the employees that had attended Arizona University, as per the request:

```
SELECT COUNT (*)
FROM EMPTAB
WHERE SCHOOL = "ARIZ'
```

In this case, the query can be satisfied entirely in the index without having to access the primary data. Much I/O is saved by satisfying this request in the index.

	EMP NO	DATE ATTENDED	SCHOOL	DEGREE	MAJOR
page 1	1456	1967	Yale	---	Math
	1456	1970	Arizona	BS	Math
	1456	1972	Arizona	MS	Comp Sci
	1459	1981	Miami	BS	Business
	--------	-------	----------	---	----------
page 2	1701	1968	UCLA	BS	Civil Eng
	1714	1979	Harvard	BS	English
	1714	1984	U Texas	MS	English
	1743	1980	U Colorado	---	Anthropology
	1752	1963	Dartmouth	BS	Spanish
	-------	-------	-----------	---	----------

SCHOOL INDEX

ARIZ	ARIZ	ARIZ	ARIZ	ARIZ	ARIZ	----------
pg01	pg01	pg04	pg10	pg12	pg 16	----------
ent1	ent1	ent2	ent6	ent7	ent6	----------

HARV	HARV	HOFS	HOFS	HOFS	ILST	----------
pg02	pg10	pg09	pg07	pg15	pg12	----------
ent2	ent1	ent5	ent6	ent4	ent3	----------

FIGURE 10. An index on school allows the employee education table to be accessed directly based on the school.

As useful as indexes are in saving I/O in the access of data, indexes have a corresponding cost as the data that is indexed changes and needs to be updated and at the point in time that the data needs to be loaded. Consider the simple table in Figure 11.

The table in Figure 11 shows the department in which an employee works. There is an index on department that shows the department of an employee.

Consider the I/O that occurs when an employee changes depart-

EMP NO	DEPT
1456	43J
1607	14BR
1995	QA1
0121	43J

DEPARTMENT/EMPLOYEE INDEX

DEPT	001A	001A	001A	001A	001C	----------
EMPNO	0081	0094	0189	0776	0018	----------
PAGE	0010	0016	0089	0098	0097	----------
ROWID	0001	0002	0001	0003	0003	----------

FIGURE 11. A table showing the department in which an employee works and an index on the employees in the department.

ments. One I/O must be done to retrieve the data in the primary data base. Another I/O is done to update the primary data. Another I/O must be done to delete the index reference from the old department. Still another I/O must be done to the index to insert the reference to the employee's new department. In all, four I/Os are required to accommodate the change of departments. If there were no index by department, only two I/Os would have been needed to accommodate the change in data. In general, when data that is indexed undergoes change, two I/Os per index are required to keep the data current in addition to the I/O required for normal update of the data.

The application designer must take into consideration the amount of work done by the system in order to load the index. As a table is loaded, each indexed column requires one I/O for the loading of the index. Of course, an index can be created at any time, not just at the moment when the data base is being loaded. But the utilities provided for loading are such that loading the index at the time that the data base is initially created is most usually efficient.

Another consideration of indexes concerns indexing on data values that occur frequently. For example, in a personnel file, employees may be classified as exempt or nonexempt (having a field content of E or N). Creating an index on a commonly occurring value such as exempt or nonexempt is probably wasteful. When searches need to be done based on the value, it is most likely faster to actually access each page, row by row, than it is to access the data on an index. Each data page will likely be read anyway so index processing is just wasted work done by the system.

The designer must be constantly aware of the I/O requirements at update, creation, and deletion time, which are traded off for access efficiency.

But there is another pitfall in the usage of indexes, and that is in using an index for a wholesale reversal of the order of the data. It is very expensive to use an index to access an entire data base in its indexed order. Suppose an automobile parts table has been loaded so that data is colocated on parts number. This means that the parts are physically grouped together based on their key value. Suppose that in addition to a key on parts, there is a key on the column unit of measure. Figure 12 shows the simple arrangement of data and indexes.

Now suppose an application analyst wishes to access the entire PARTS table based on the value of the unit of measure. The unit of measure index is used, beginning at the first entry, then the next, and so forth. How much I/O is consumed by this process?

In general, each entry that is accessed goes to a different location. Looking at the first row referenced by the index causes block 1098 to be accessed. The next row causes block 8907 to be accessed, and so forth. In other words, by using the unit of measure index to reorder the PARTS table, one I/O per entry index is required (ignoring the occasional fortuitous buffer hit).

The result is that indexes should be used for limited entry. When this practice is not followed, the result is very poor performance.

REFERENTIAL INTEGRITY

Referential integrity is the capability of a system to keep the relationships between two occurrences of data synchronized in the face of change when data is interrelated by means of a foreign key. ORACLE Version 6.0 depends upon the application programmer to implement and maintain referential integrity. ORACLE, of course, uses foreign keys to relate different tables together, as shown in Figure 13.

Figure 13 shows a simple relationship in which two tables—a

	PART NO	DESC	QTY	U/M
BLOCK 1098	1209-a	Cam Shift	290	P
	1301-s	Gear Shift	24	P
	1410-a	Bots-#34	22304	B
	12108	Nuts - #321	3409	B
BLOCK 8907	1209-b	Idler Arm	34	P
	1209-f	Rocker Assem	23	B
	1209-g	Filter-343	32	P
	1208	Engine	34	B

PART INDEX

PART	1208	1209-a	1209-b	1209-f	1209-g	1301-s
block	8907	1098	8907	8907	8907	1098
entry	0004	0001	0001	0002	0003	0002

FIGURE 12. A simple arrangement of data and indexes for a PARTS table.

PARTS table and a SUPPLIER SHIPMENT table—are related. The supplier shipment table contains the key—partno—indicating which partno the shipment has supplied. The relationship is invalid when a partno is entered into the shipment data base that is not in the parts table. The application programmer is charged with keeping the contents and the validity of the relationship between the two tables in order.

Consider another more complex relationship, as shown by Figure 14.

Figure 14 shows three ORACLE tables: a PARTS table, a SUPPLIER table, and a SUPPLIER/PART NUMBER cross-reference table. Consider what happens when part number 10087-pw is deleted from the PARTS table. For the system to remain "pure," all references to part number 10087-pw must be immediately (i.e., in the same transaction) deleted in all the tables that reference part number. In the example shown, the supplier/parts cross reference would need to

PART NO	AMT	DESC	U/M
1897ty-9	560	manifold	unit
776t-908	10700	base plate	tub
66509-u	56	housing mold	unit
10087-pw	600900	bearings	tub
9978-rtw2	6700	platform	unit
------------	-------	------------	-------

SHIPMENT	PART NO	QTY	DATE	LOCATION
1110900-a	9978-rtw2	9008000	01/01/89	Sunnyvale
220908-as	92256-po	90822	12/15/87	San Jose
233098-1a	77265-s	2120000	10/11/88	San Leandro
3334000r	44445-a	34678	08/12/89	San Diego
-------------	----------	----------	------------	------------

FIGURE 13. A simple relationship between tables.

have the Jones Hardware reference for that part deleted. If the cross reference is not deleted, then the cross reference will show that Jones Hardware is the supplier of a nonexistent part.

From a performance perspective, there are several options in the management of referential integrity. One option is to delete all references to a part when the part is deleted as an integral element of the online transaction. Unfortunately, this might require much I/O in the middle of the online day, thus causing a major performance difficulty. However, repairing the logical inconsistency "on the spot" keeps the data of the system "pure."

If absolute purity (i.e., up-to-the-second accuracy) is not required, then another strategy is to wait until the peak hours of processing have passed and then repair the inconsistency in the data base. The transaction that has deleted the part keeps track of the fact that it has executed successfully and is stored with other transactions that have likewise executed successfully. Then, during nonpeak hours, those transactions are batched together and run against the tables that relate

PART NO	AMT	DESC	U/M
1897ty-9	560	manifold	unit
776t-908	10700	base plate	tub
66509-u	56	housing mold	unit
10087-pw	600900	bearings	tub
9978-rtw2	6700	platfom	unit
----------	-------	----------	------

SUPPLIER	ADDRESS	CONTACT	PHONE
Jones Hrdware	123 Main St	J Cash	990-8879
Emporium	90 Broad	J Carter	889-0098
Wilson Store	13 First, 10th	R Acuff	990-9982
Pace Whse	1 S Jefferson St	R Clark	990-9908
------------	----------------	-----------	-----------
------------	----------------	-----------	-----------

SUPPLIER/PART NUMBER	
Jones Hdware	10087-pw
Jones Hdware	887-yt65
Jones Hdware	9887-uyu
Jones Hdware	9987-ppo
Pace Whse	776t-908
Pace Whse	880-uyti
--------------	----------
--------------	----------

FIGURE 14. Three relational tables — a PARTS table, a SUPPLIER table, and a cross-reference table.

to data bases that have been updated during peak-hour processing. Figure 15 illustrates these two options.

Even though relationships are built and controlled at the application, and in theory there will never be an error, it is good practice to build utilities at the application level that verify the validity of the relationships. This utility is run from time to time, making sure that every relationship is valid. Because the utility accesses all the data in the data bases participating in the relationship, other worthwhile information can be collected as the utility is run. Information about the data bases can be collected as a matter of course, such as:

- Number of rows participating in relationships.
- Number of occurrences of data in the average, in the worse case, etc, participating in a 1:n relationship.

The application designer should keep two things in mind in the building of relationships between tables:

- Overhead
- Complexity

The application designer must keep in mind at all times that work—I/O—is required by the system in order to keep referential integrity relationships in order. And a second consideration is complexity. As a rule, the more straightforward and the fewer relationships there are, the smoother the development process will be, not to mention the operations environment after the application has gone into production.

LARGE TABLES

It is normal for data managed by a DBMS to occur many times. For example, a customer table may have 100,000 rows, or a PARTS table may have 10,000 parts. Such are the realities of handling data under a DBMS. But occasionally data occurs in large enough numbers that special design techniques are required. For example, suppose a bank has 100,000 customers and suppose each customer has, on the average, 25 banking activities each month. Now suppose the bank wishes to store five years worth of history per customer in an ORACLE data base. The number of rows to be stored, then, is:

$$100{,}000 \times 25 \times 12 \times 5 = 150{,}000{,}000 \text{ rows}$$

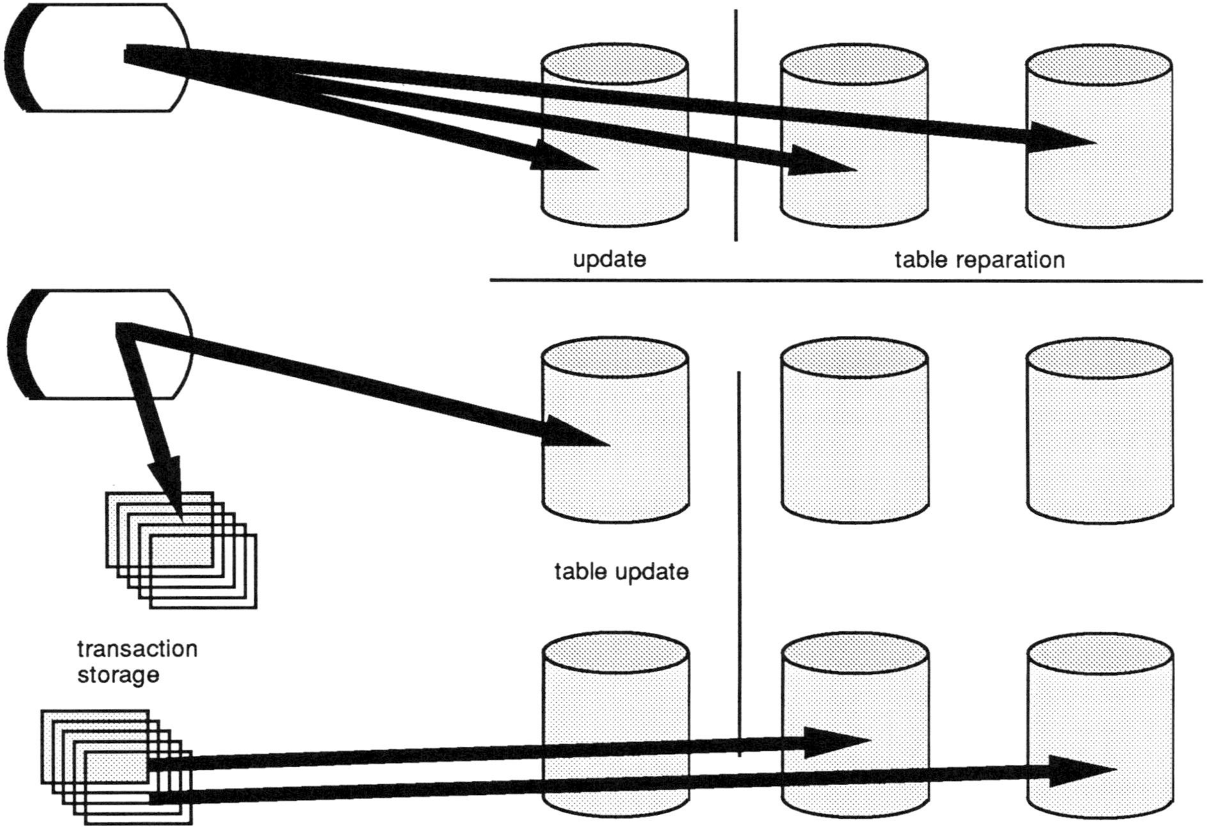

FIGURE 15. Transaction reparation during nonpeak hours.

By anyone's criteria and under anyone's storage mechanism, that is a lot of data!

The first question to be asked is:

Is it necessary to keep all that data in a data base?

An interesting analysis can be made of the probability of access of the data. With 150,000,000 rows of data stored, how many will ever be used, and what is the cost of the storage? The first issue that must be settled is:

What data can be weaned out because it will never be accessed?

Suppose, however, that all the data is kept. What are the design options? One approach would be to create one row for each customer activity, as shown by the data base design in Figure 16.

A word of explanation is in order for this table. The key is customer number, date, and activity number. Activity number is required to force uniqueness of the key. Without activity number, any customer

CUST NO	YR/	MO/	DA	LOC	AMOUNT
3341-0	86	06	12	AZS	136.20
3341-0	86	06	12	AZS	1080.87
3341-0	86	06	12	AZS	73.97
3341-0	86	06	25	AZS	124.56
3981-8	86	06	11	FRW	760.00
3981-8	86	06	14	FRW	450.65
3981-8	86	06	15	FRW	100.00
3981-8	86	06	17	FRW	18.89
3981-8	86	06	18	FRW	90.00
3981-8	86	06	15	HGA	1000.00
---------	---	---	---	-------	--------

FIGURE 16. A simple table where data is highly normalized.

doing more than one business activity on the same day would create nonunique keys. While this approach to data base design is simple, it carries with it some problems that can hamper system performance and availability. If the data is nonclustered, consider the number of index entries required—with one index entry for each row, i.e., 150,000,000 index entries are required for each index. That is a large amount of data even for indexed access.

But access of data is not the only problem.

Consider the work required of the system when the definition of a given field needs to be modified. The new definition of the data must be presented to the system. Then the field must be unloaded in its old format and reloaded in its new format. If the field has an index, the index must be recreated. In short the sheer volume-of data to be manipulated in the redefinition of data presents its own special problems that arise solely because of the volume of data.

Now consider what would happen if common usage of the data dictated that several day's banking activities for a customer needed to be accessed, as illustrated by the following request: For customer 1234, retrieve all banking activity for the week of July 20, 1986, to July 27, 1986. Locating the index records does not require a (relatively!) large amount of I/O because the index is tightly packed and contains several levels. But what about the I/O required to access the rows of data?

The first row is in page 99, the next row is in page 32, the next in page 45, and so forth. (In other words, even though the index is compactly arranged and efficient to traverse in terms of I/O consumption, the data pointed to by the index is widely dispersed and requires much I/O for its access). Going from one row to the next requires one I/O per row (because each row is in a physically different page), and for a significant number of rows, the I/O consumed mounts quickly.

Now suppose the table was clustered. This means that going from one row to the next does not require I/O in order to retrieve data with related key values unless, of course, a new page is encountered. And there are fewer index entries for the index pointing to the primary key. So clustering of data is the first step towards managing a large amount of data.

But there are other design options that can be utilized as well. One such option is depicted by Figure 17.

There are several features of the design in Figure 17 that enhance performance. The primary key of the table shown in Figure 17 is customer number, year/month of activity, location, and group number. Following the key are up to five occurrences of data, showing actual

CUST NO	YR/ MO	LOC	GROUP	1st DAY	1st AMT	2nd DAY	2nd AMT	3rd DAY	3rd AMT -----
3341-0	8606	AZS	00001	12	136.20	12	1080.87	23	73.97
3981-8	8606	FRW	00001	11	760.00	14	458.65	15	100.00
3981-8	8606	FRW	00002	18	90.00	19	15.00	21	100.00
3981-8	8606	HGA	00001	15	1000.00	---	-------	---	-------
----------	-------	-------	--------	---	-------	---	-------	---	-------

FIGURE 17. A different arrangment of customer activity data that packs the data more tightly. The effectiveness of this approach depends on a knowledge of the customer's data and the activity and habits of the customer.

date of the month of the activity and the amount of the activity. When there are less than five occurrences of activities of the same key, null values are used. When there are more than five activities for a customer/year/month/location, then a new group of activities is created, thus building a new row with a unique key. In this case group number is incremented by one.

Some of the efficiencies of this structuring of data include:

- Many fewer index entries, regardless of whether the rows are clustered or not. Roughly one-fourth of the index entries will be needed in the example shown because of the grouping of activity entries.
- Data is compacted. Redundant occurrences of data, such as month and year, have been eliminated. The result is physically less data.
- Once a row is in the buffer, all five occurrences of data will be accessible in every case. Processing up to five activities at a time requires only one I/O.

The effectiveness of the design depends greatly on the knowledge of a customer's habits and the usage of the data in the table. For example, if a customer frequents many different locations to execute banking activities, then this structuring of data may actually cost performance and space; each time a customer goes to a new location, a new row is created. But as long as customers are creatures of habit and have their own favorite tellers or ATMs, then the structuring of data, as depicted, saves both space and I/O.

The selection of the number of occurrences that should fit into any row is not a random selection. The number of occurrences in each row in the case of the example shown in Figure 17 depends upon:

- The physical block size into which the row must fit.
- The number of occurrences of data—the average and the standard deviation.
- The pattern of access of data—random, sequential, etc.
- The pattern of insertions and deletions.
- The inability to directly index an occurrence once the occurrence has entered a row.

The designer, then, has a number of options that are available in the management of large numbers of rows, in addition to clustering data.

Another design technique is the wholesale division of data into separate tables.

Oftentimes, when there is a large amount of data, it makes sense to organize it into collections that are active or inactive (i.e., archived). An active data base is one that contains data with a high probability of access. An archival data base is one that contains data with a low probability of access, usually containing nonrecent historical data. By separating the two types of data during design, the designer circumvents many problems during implementation.

One technique for the management of active and archival data is the placement of active data on the fastest storage device available and the placement of archival data on slower storage devices or devices that are geared for handling massive amounts of data. In such a manner, the hierarchy of storage is matched with the usage of data.

One useful criterion for determining when data should and should not be archived is whether it makes sense to update the data. Generally speaking, when data has the potential to be updated it should not be archived, and when data does not need to be updated (or has a very low probability of being updated) it may be archived. This division of data fits ingeniously with the data management technology found in both the operational and archival environments (i.e., operational technology is geared for update and archival technology is not). For a large collection of data, it is not unusual to have 5 percent of the data in the active data base and 95 percent of the data in the archival data base. The separation of data makes set-at-a-time processing of data viable.

In the example being discussed, suppose a bank divided customer activity into two groups of data. One group of activity data is for the most current activity—activity occurring in the past 60 days. All other activity is placed in another data base, with activity going back two to three years. In such a manner, the data that is kept online—the most current data—is reduced to a manageable size.

In some cases, a useful technique in the archiving of data, where data is stored in separate locations, is to create an I/O module that knows the location of data. Thus, the actual location is masked from the programmer.

But separating large amounts of data according to archival needs is only one way to break up large collections of data. There are many other criteria that can be used for separation. Some of them follow.

- Separation by function. Instead of a parts data base that contains many rows, several data bases can be formed, each of which is smaller than the collective data base but which, taken together, logically comprise the large collection of data. A drive train data base, a body data base, an interior data base, a steering data base, etc., can be created so that all of the assembly is represented, but in different tables. ORACLE can allow the data to be distributed over different processors and still allow the query to be processed.

- Separation by key range. Suppose a parts data base needs to be physically subdivided into smaller tables. One table contains parts whose key begins with '0.' The next table contains keys whose first digit is '1,' and so forth. In such a manner a large data base can arbitrarily be split into multiple data bases.
- Separation by date. Suppose an archival data base is to be created. The archived data can be separated by year, by year/month, by year/month/day, and so forth. The granularity of the split depends on the amount of data and the usage of data.
- Separation by geographical division. A retail vendor can either have a single large customer data base or several smaller data bases that segment the customers according to geographic location. The retailer may have, for example, a Northern California data base, a Southern California data base, a Central California data base, and so on.
- Separation by customer classification. A bank can have a single accounts data base, or it may choose to have the accounts broken up by customer classification, such as commercial accounts, individual accounts (active), individual accounts (inactive), individual accounts –upscale, etc.

From the above examples it is obvious that the data base designer can segment large collections of data in many different ways. Given the set processing orientation and distributed query processing capability of ORACLE's SQL, segmentation has many advantages.

Some guidelines for the designer in the selection of the proper criteria for separation or segmentation include:

- Are the categories chosen for separation mutually exclusive? If not, more than one occurrence of data may fit in multiple categories. (If an occurrence of data fits in more than one category, then the integrity of duplicate data must be maintained at the application level, something normally not desired.)
- Will the categorization effectively reduce the size of the data bases? On occasion, subcategorization appears to reduce the size of the data

bases, but an analysis at the physical level shows that only a small reduction is being achieved. When the bulk of data is not reduced by subcategorization, nearly all data fits into a single subcategory.

- Will the subcategorization of one data base fit with the subcategorization criteria of another data base? For example, if in an insurance company all customers are subdivided by geographic region, it may be difficult to subdivide all accounts by other criteria, such as upscale, commercial, active, etc., customers.

There are, then, a variety of design techniques the designer can use in the management of large amounts of data. These techniques include:

- Clustering data
- Creating arrays within a row
- Separating archival data from active data
- Subdividing data on other criteria

VARIABLE-LENGTH COLUMNS

One option the data base designer has with ORACLE is variable-length columns. Of course, any character data type in ORACLE can vary in length. However, some columns consistently contain lengths that never vary and other columns contain data whose length varies widely. ORACLE states that after release 6.0 differentiation may be made between CHAR and VARCHAR. The proper design and use of variable-length columns as opposed to columns whose length does not vary is important to performance because their improper use can lead to unnecessary I/O. In addition, the management of variable-length columns requires a certain amount of CPU overhead. Another cost incurred is the overhead of storage required for each variable column.

A variable-length column is one that can have different lengths for different occurrences of data. Names and text are common candidates for variable-length columns. As a simple example, suppose the designer has specified NAME as a column in a table. Then the name JEANNE FRIEDMAN will require 15 bytes of information for its occurrence as a variable-length column, and the name TF CHANG will require 8 bytes of information for its occurrence as a variable-length column.

There is nothing wrong, per se, with variable-length columns as far as performance is concerned, but instances can arise where they can cause much CPU and I/O to be consumed. Consider the following example. The name JEANNE FRIEDMAN exists in a table as an occurrence of a variable-length column. Jeanne Friedman marries and decides to take the name of her husband, James Sylvester. The programmer retrieves the name JEANNE FRIEDMAN and wishes to replace it with the name JEANNE SYLVESTER. So far, no unnecessary amount of I/O has been expended. But upon trying to replace 16 bytes where there once were 15 presents an opportunity for I/O. I/O is used when the extra byte cannot be accommodated upon replacement by available free space in the block.

If the data is loosely packed (i.e., packed with much free space) there probably is no data management required. But if it is tightly packed, then, at the very least, the row containing the name JEANNE SYLVESTER must be replaced within the block. But there may not be room for the new row in the block and another block must be located where there is available space. Locating that block and adjusting the index does require I/O.

The converse design problem—that of replacing smaller variable-length columns than what was originally retrieved—does not cost I/O but does cost space in the data base that cannot be easily retrieved. For example, suppose Jeanne Friedman married Fred Smith and decided to change her name. To reclaim the space under normal circumstances requires a data base reorganization. For all practical purposes, the ORACLE page has lost three bytes of data until the next reorganization. While this loss of data in and of itself is small, when data is volatile and is constantly being churned, the loss adds up.

One caution is that variable-length columns can cost I/O or wasted space when, once created, they are allowed to be updated. Of course, if the length of the occurrence of data in the column is established at the moment of creation of the row and never changes, then there is no performance conflict. For example, suppose a title company wishes to list the street address of properties it manages along with other information about the property. Once the street address is written, it is highly unlikely that the address will ever change. But the amount of storage used for one property description and another differs dramatically, so a variable column definition is in order. The stability of the description is such that the occurrence of data in the column, once created, is very unlikely to change, thus minimizing the problems with I/O or wasted space.

The ORACLE physical data base design option PCTFREE can be used to alleviate some of the problems of variable-length rows. PCTFREE is used in the loading of a table and indicates the amount of free space (in terms of percentages) that is to be left unused after the loading of the first record. If the designer anticipates variable rows with a high degree of volatility, then free space can be left. If, however, the space becomes used or otherwise unavailable, a reorganization of the data must be done to reallocate free space. Note that PCTUSED, another related ORACLE physical data base design option does nothing to alleviate the problems of variable rows flowing beyond the boundary of a single page when the size of a variable-length field changes. It does, however, allow recovery of space freed by deletes for use by inserts.

Once ORACLE distinguishes between CHAR and VARCHAR, another consideration of physical data base design in regard to variable-length columns is the positioning of the variable-length column within the row. If all the columns are laid from right to left, the variable-length columns must be positioned to the right of the fixed-length columns. The reason for this rather arbitrary rule of thumb is that columns of data are accessed based on their physical address. First the row of data is located, then the columns within the row are located. All fixed-length columns can be easily located by calculating an offset from the first of the row, but columns appearing after a variable-length column must have their address calculated by means of determining how long the variable-length column is.

Suppose there were five columns: A, B, C, D, and E, in that order in a table. Suppose that A, B, D, and E are fixed length. Locating the address of columns A and B is easy. Find the beginning of the row and A and B are always the same distance from it. In fact, finding the start of column C is easy as well because all the rows preceding it are fixed length. But finding the starting address of D and E requires that the length of C be calculated for every access of the row.

To summarize, the designer needs to be careful in the update and manipulation of variable-length columns. In addition, the designer needs to be aware that the physical positioning of the columns within the row may or may not require system overhead in the accessing of any column in the row.

CONTROL DATA BASES

While most relational tables contain data that is directly related to an application, such as customer, account, part number data, it is frequently useful to put data that can be considered auxiliary (or utilitarian) in a relational table as well. This type of data base can be called a "control data base" and typically holds security data, audit data, table data, terminal data, etc. There is nothing wrong, per se, with control data bases. But they are often candidates for performance and availability bottlenecks. (Note: the control data bases being discussed should not be confused with ORACLE's control files.)

Because control data bases contain utilitarian information, they tend to be widely used. Because they are widely used, there is often much competition to get at the data in the control data base. The competition is elevated when update of control data bases occurs.

In addition, the effect of a control data base going down can be catastrophic because the data bases are so widely used. When the control data base goes down, users cannot accomplish their work until it is brought back up. And because the control data base is so popular, many transactions and programs are disabled by taking it offline.

One of the reasons control data bases cause problems is the locking of data.

One of the online features of ORACLE is locking of data. Locking prevents two online users from accessing and updating the same data at the same time. Locking in ORACLE can occur at different levels —from the row level up to the tablespace level. Assuming that most developers building production systems will have the transaction processing option, all locks will be at the row level unless explicitly locked at the table level for administrative tasks. Furthermore, locking can be done "exclusively" or "shared." When locking is exclusive no other program can access the data while the data is locked. When shared, read-only access of the data is allowed while the data is locked.

Figure 18 shows that user A has accessed and is updating (or at least has the potential for updating) a terminal security table (one form of a control data base). In the example shown, locking is exclusive and at the row level.

While user A is controlling the terminal security data base, user B must wait. The two users are in contention for the same data at the same time, and the system is essentially single threaded. User A must free the terminal security data for user B to be able to continue processing.

There are several solutions to the problems presented by control data bases at the design level. They depend upon the needs of the application.

An easy solution is to specify locking at the row level. Only when two users actually want access to the very same row will contention occur. But locking at the row level every time the control data base is accessed may entail a high degree of overhead.

Another solution is to duplicate the data in the terminal security data base, as shown by Figure 19.

In this case, when user A wishes to access and update the terminal

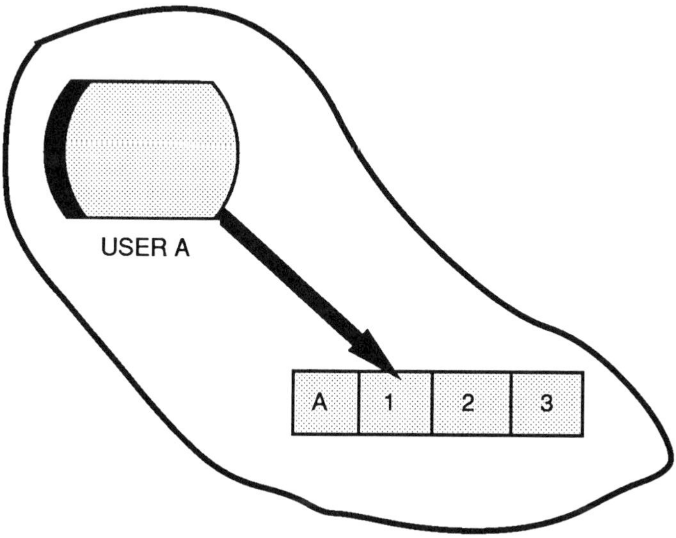

FIGURE 18. Lockout occurs when user A and user B are attempting to access and update the same row of data in the terminal security table at the same time.

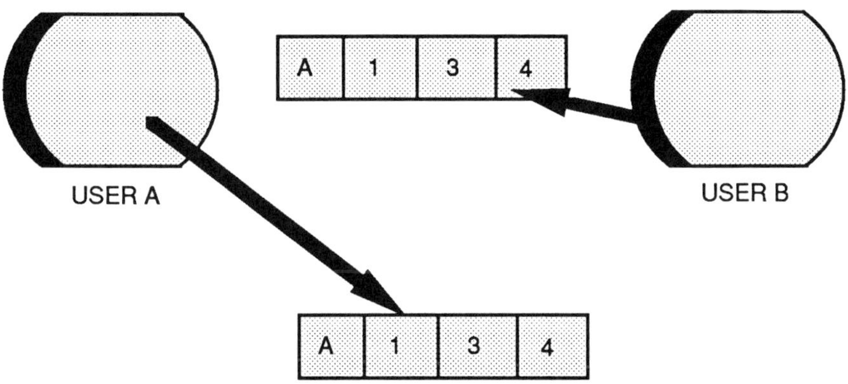

FIGURE 19. One solution to the locking dilemma is to duplicate the data if the application will allow.

security data, there is no contention with user B because user B is accessing a copy of the data being held by user A, not the actual data. This solution depends, of course, upon the fact that the terminal security data can be duplicated, which is often not the case.

Another option is to subdivide the terminal security data into small units of access (i.e., create only a few columns in each table) and physically separate the data (i.e., creating physically separate tables or separating different types of data into separate tables), as shown in Figure 20.

In Figure 20, there is no contention between users A and B because the users are after different parts of the terminal security data base. The design techniques of separation and replication can be used, of course, for noncontrol data bases, where contention and locking are potential problems.

It is worth noting that the techniques discussed for the management of control data have their downside. Duplicating data and breaking it down into very fine divisions have implications of integrity, update, program development and maintenance, and so forth.

DATA VIEWS

One feature of ORACLE is data views (or simply "views"). A view is nothing more than a logical perspective of data, as opposed to a physical perspective of data. Figure 21 shows a typical ORACLE view of account data and activity.

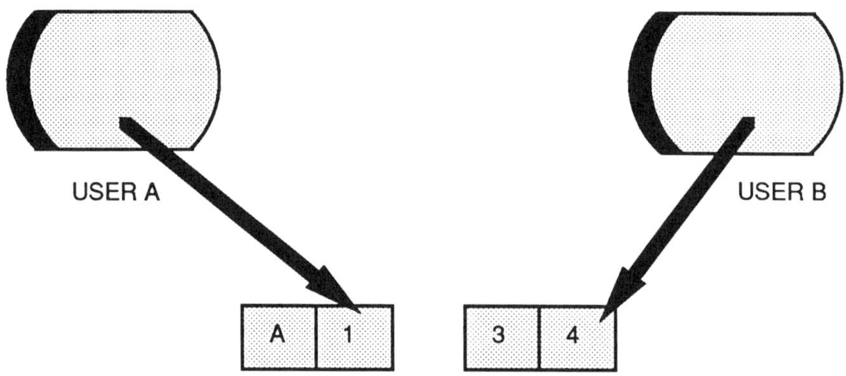

FIGURE 20. Separating data at the point of design is another solution to the dilemma posed by lockout.

ACCT	DATE OPENED	LOCATION	BALANCE
1456	741223	Burlingame	596.92
1984	790813	San Mateo	11662.45
9721	810115	Sunnyvale	26.62
0112	860720	San Jose	1340.21
-------	------------	--------------	--------

ACCT	ACTIVITY DATE	AMOUNT	FORM
0112	860901	13.14	EFT
0112	860902	29.36	EFT
0112	860902	1000.00	TJM
0112	860909	78.41	EFT
0112	860910	(2553.40)	EFT
0112	860912	75.00	TJM
-------	---------	-------	-------

FIGURE 21. A view of data—the account information and the activity for Sept 10 are joined. The view spans two tables.

Views can be useful for creating distinct, easily perceived perspectives of data. But from a performance standpoint, views can be harmful to performance when the background work done by the system is factored into the view. When a view spans two or more tables, a large amount of I/O may be required to service it. On one hand, the view appears as a simple structuring of data to the user; on the other hand, the view may require large amounts of I/O to be consumed as the system constructs the view in the background. As a result the designer should be careful in the assignment and usage of views. Generally speaking, the designer is safest with presenting data as it is defined in its table.

When views do not span multiple tables, they may actually enhance performance. Consider the table shown in Figure 22.

ACCT	OPENED	LOCATION	BALANCE	OPTIONS	ID
1456	740712	Burlingame	586.52	AQR	1585
1984	790813	San Mateo	11662.87	------	JU72
9721	810101	Sunnyvale	26.62	ARM	3081
0112	860720	Palo Alto	137.78	AD	4381
0998	790818	Mountain View	2234.78	------	IP
9883	771019	San Carlos	12.55	AR	PPi
9887	770812	Belmont	1200.00	AQR	100P
9802	781019	Fremont	15000.09	ARD	099L
-------	-----------	-------------	--------	------	------

FIGURE 22. A view of data that does not span two tables.

Suppose the fields—account, date opened, and location—were indexed and the remaining fields in the table were not. The view allows the user to access the table only on fields that are quickly and efficiently retrievable (other than indexing on balance, which is a questionable field for indexing in any case). Because a subset of data is chosen that does not span multiple tables and that does not allow access or retrieval on nonindexed fields, a view may actually enhance performance.

SEQUENTIALLY ACCESSING DATA

ORACLE data can be accessed randomly. If there is only a small amount of data to be handled, the issue of the basic access path is not terribly important. But in the face of large amounts of data, the designer must carefully influence the basic access path because much I/O can be wasted if the designer fails to make the correct choice.

The first method of organizing ORACLE data is in an unclustered, indexed fashion, as shown by Figure 23.

The index in Figure 23 is sequenced and points to data, which is itself randomly organized. Unclustered data is ideal for online transaction processing that must access a single row of data at a time, satisfying such online activity as "What is the quantity on hand of part 20156?"

	PART	DESC	QTY	U/M	CLASS
page 1	165	Screw	13	tub	np
	-----	-------	---	-----	-----
	20156	Bolt	1590	tub	nop
	1A-6	Housing	2	unit	p

page 2	453	nut	260	tub	np
	-----	-------	---	-----	-----
	-----	-------	---	-----	-----
	1A-1	body	25	unit	p

PART NO INDEX

PART NO	165	1A-1	1A-6	453	20156
rowid	page1	page2	page1	page2	page1

FIGURE 23. Index entries into unclustered data.

But if more than one row of data is regularly required (especially if many rows of data are required) then accessing ORACLE unclustered, indexed data may cost many I/Os, as the satisfaction of one row request through the index to the next may cause an I/O for each row requested.

A second design option is to cluster data, so that as many row requests can be satisfied as possible by the accessing of a block of data. In other words, when data is clustered, an I/O is done to retrieve a row. But to retrieve the next row, and the next, and so on, no more I/Os are needed as long as the rows are in the same block and the block is being held in the buffer area. In ORACLE, different kinds of data from different tables can be physically stored in the same location based on a common key value. If rows are arranged in a manner meaningful to the application processing, a minimal amount of I/O is needed. Consider the data in Figure 24.

If clustering of data can save I/O upon access, shouldn't all tables be clustered? The answer is no, because upon insertion of data or update of data in the case of variable-length rows, clustering can actually cost I/O. For example, suppose the row for the part number 1A-5 were to be inserted into a data base but there is no room for it. As a consequence part of the data in the block must be moved to other blocks and the result is more I/O required for data management.

Clustering, then, can be used to optimally arrange data in a physical sequence that is good for frequent joined access. But only one physical optimization of data is possible (because a table or tables can be clustered only once), even though the data may be accessed any number of ways.

	PART	DESC	QTY	U/M	CLASS
page 1	165	Screw	13	tub	np
	1A-1	body	25	unit	p
	1A-6	Housing	2	unit	p
	20156	Bolt	1590	tub	nop
Page 2	453	nut	260	tub	np
	-----	-------	---	-----	-----
	-----	-------	---	-----	-----
	-----	-------	---	-----	-----

PART NO INDEX

PART NO	165	1A-1	1A-6	20156	453
ROWID	page1	page2	page1	page1	page2

FIGURE 24. Index entries into clustered data.

ENCODING OF DATA

Another application design option is the encoding of data. Encoding is useful for saving space and, on some occasions, for the savings of I/O. But encoding costs CPU resources and often costs I/O. When there is a need to go from the encoded value to its transformation, I/O is used.

The fewer tables, the fewer occasions to have to join or otherwise dynamically interconnect relational data. And the fewer interconnections made, the better performance is. One opportunity the designer has to minimize the number of tables without compromising the design of the system is to avoid encoded data.

A simple example of an encoded value would be the one byte of storage in a table denoting either male or female, F or M. Another form of simple encoding might be a value of 1, 2, or 3 in a table where:

1–Headquarters, New York, New York,
2–Branch Office, Detroit Michigan
3–Field Office, El Paso, Texas

In general, when encoded values are used, there is no need for the programmer or the user to go from the encoded value to its transformation and in doing so use I/O. When there is no need to go to the encoded value, no I/O is used and there is no performance problem. But when there is a need to go from the encoded table to the encoded value, I/O is used and performance suffers. For that reason, the fewer the encoded values there, the better. Of course, where there is a small, stable number of values, the DECODE operator can be used.

Encoded values as an application design technique are not quite as straightforward as the declaration that they should never be used, however. The designer should consider the following.

- Some encoded values are universally recognizable abbreviations, such as F for female and M for male. When encoded values are self-evident they can save space and require no I/O because they do not need to be translated.
- Some encoded values are so commonly used within a company that a transformation from the encoded value to the actual value will seldom take place. In this case encoding requires minimal I/O and has no effect on performance,
- Retrievals requiring translation (i.e., lookup in separate tables) may be a small percentage of total retrievals required in processing the

row. For example, a human resources system may encode job class to save space in each row, but only rarely will the printing of the actual job class be required.

- Encoding can save I/O in some cases. Suppose the headquarters of a company is at one location and is encoded as "Hdqtr" throughout the system. When the headquarters is moved from Ithaca, New York, to Buffalo, New York, the change in address need be made in only one place. All encoded references are still valid even though the actual value has changed,
- The length of data of the encoded transformation may vary widely. This may (or may not) present special data management problems. When the data is encoded, the data management problems are minimized because the encoded values are uniformly short.

From the above discussion it is clear that whether to encode or not is a product of many factors. In general, encoding may cost I/O, but there may exist special circumstances in which encoding offers other benefits that more than compensate for the I/O that might be consumed.

SUMMARY

The first physical data base design issue the application designer faces is indexing data. Whether to index, how to index, and avoiding overhead are all considerations of physical data base design.

Another issue the physical designer faces is referential integrity, which in ORACLE is entirely up to the application programmer. Referential integrity can be an impediment to performance and must be designed keeping in mind the underlying physical I/Os that are required.

Large data bases require special handling for reasons of performance and availability. In general, large collections of data should be broken up into multiple smaller collections.

Clustering of data is another physical design issue that is especially appropriate to the management of large data bases.

Variable-length columns have their own performance implications. When a variable-length column is accessed and replaced with more data than was present when the variable column was accessed, then I/O may be needed for data management in the storage of the variable-length column.

Control data bases can become a bottleneck to performance when one or more applications are forced to single-thread through a control data base that is being updated. Control data can be proliferated or broken into finer units of storage in order to expedite the flow through the data base.

Encoding of data is a technique that can harm performance if used improperly. Both CPU and I/O resources are used in encoding and decoding.

QUESTIONS: PHYSICAL DATA BASE DESIGN IN ORACLE

1. Indexing can help performance by allowing data to be accessed _______________.
2. Without an index, search for a given value must be done _______________.
3. Sequential searches for data do not harm performance in the face of LARGE/SMALL data bases.
4. But most production data bases are LARGE/SMALL.
5. At least _______________ I/Os are required to access a single indexed row.
6. When a column that is indexed is altered, _______________ to the data must be changed.
7. Indexes trade off efficiency of access for efficiency of _______________.
8. Some queries can be satisfied by processing in the _______________.
9. When a value occurs MANY/FEW times, it may be more efficient to access the pages than the index.
10. When data has interrelationships, the maintenance of the relationship is known as _______________.
11. Referential integrity is done by the _______________.
12. When two tables are related and one table has a row deleted, a corresponding row MAY/MUST be deleted.
13. Tables require relationships to be kept up to date instantaneously. T/F.
14. Referential integrity may be maintained by overnight _______________ processing in some cases.
15. Performance of large data bases can be hindered because _______________ of data may not be done as frequently as needed.

16. Availability of large data bases can be hindered because ______________ of data may take a long time.

17. Reorganization and recovery can be enhanced by REDUCING/INCREASING the amount of data in a data base.

18. Reducing the amount of data in a data base NECESSARILY IMPLIES/DOES NOT NECESSARILY IMPLY less data to be managed by ORACLE.

19. Logically relating data, while reducing the physical size of any component, ENHANCES/HURTS reorganization/recovery needs.

20. Data that is seldom accessed is the first candidate for removal from the production environment. (T/F)

21. Archival data is often ______________ from the production environment.

22. Data can be split by ______________ range.

23. Key range splits can be done by ______________.

24. Splitting of data by key does not affect processes that access ______________ rows.

25. Splitting of data by key may have a negative effect on processes that access ______________ rows of a data base.

26. Not only rows, but ______________ entries are a factor in large data bases.

27. Using an index to sequence data requires ______________ I/Os per index entry.

28. Massive resequencing of a data base by means of an index SHOULD/SHOULD NOT be done online.

29. Clustering of data WILL/WILL NOT reduce the number of index entries.

30. One form of denormalization is creating rows with multiple occurrences of data. Multiple occurrences are ALWAYS/FREQUENTLY more tightly packed than if one entry per row existed.

31. Creating rows with multiple occurrences of data can WASTE/SAVE space and I/Os.

32. Creating rows with multiple occurrences saves space when the occurrences are uniform for every key of the row (T/F)

33. Creating rows with multiple occurrences wastes space when the occurrences are random for every key of the row. (T/F)

34. Many FEWER/MORE index entries are required when multiple occurrences of data are packed into a row.

35. Total data base space is usually SAVED/LOST by placing multiple occurrences of data in a row.

36. Some of the factors that determine whether multiple occurrences of data in a row is a good design choice are ______________.

37. Archival data is data that will never need to be accessed again. (T/F)

38. The future use of archival data is generally KNOWN/UNKNOWN.

39. Generally speaking, archival data is data that MAY/MAY NOT be updated.

40. There are two kinds of archival processing. They are ______________.

41. Generally speaking, there is ______________ data in the archival environment.

42. Archival data is stored at the LOWEST/HIGHEST level of detail.

43. Archival data can be placed on a SLOWER/FASTER media.

44. Text, names, addresses are often stored in the form of a ______________.

45. There ARE/ARE NOT inherent performance difficulties with variable-length data.

46. When variable-length data is accessed at one length and extended to another length, performance may be a problem. (T/F)

47. When variable-length data is created and not updated, performance IS/IS NOT an issue.

48. When a variable-length field is accessed and updated with a smaller value, space is usually ______________.

49. Variable-length data should always be placed BEFORE/AFTER fixed-length data in a row.

50. Organizing variable-length data that will be updated with a certain amount of free space WILL SOLVE/WILL HELP BUT NOT SOLVE the problems of performance.

51. The ORACLE option ______________ can be used to alleviate some of the problems of the variable-length data.

52. PCTFREE will reserve free space in every ______________ upon loading.

53. A table not directly related to the application but still useful is called a ______________ table.

54. Name some typical control data bases.

55. Control data bases, because of their popularity and frequent usage, are ideal candidates for ______________.

56. UPDATE/ACCESS of control data bases is the worst offender in creating the enqueue condition.

57. Update of data causes the data base manager to protect individual records. (T/F)

58. Duplicating control data is a design option that is:
   a. never applicable
   b. often applicable
   c. sometimes applicable
   d. always applicable

59. When there is not much data and the data is not updated in the online environment, then duplication of control data is a viable option. (T/F)

60. Separation of data at the row level, or even the field level, MAY/PROBABLY WON'T alleviate the problems of control data bases.

61. A data view can span ______________ or more tables.

62. When a data view spans only one table, it is unlikely that performance will be an issue. (T/F)

63. When a data view spans more than one table, performance:
   a. is a problem
   b. may be a problem
   c. sometimes might be a problem
   d. is not a problem

64. The utilities for ______________ and ______________ form the basis for availability analysis.

65. When a data base fails, for whatever reason, it must be ______________.

66. It should be assumed that all online data bases, at one time or the other, are going to fail. (T/F)

67. There are a variety of reasons for reorganization of data, Some of them are ______________.

68. When a data base is being recovered or reorganized, it is ______________ for other processing.

69. The larger the data base, the LONGER/SHORTER the time required for recovery or reorganization.

70. The time required for recovery and reorganization SHOULD BE/CANNOT BE calculated prior to programming and detailed design.

71. The amount of time required for some types of recovery and reorganization can be cut by breaking data in to physically fewer units. This technique is called ______________ data.

72. Partitioning of data can be done at the ______________ or the ______________ level.

73. Partitioning will save resources in ALL/SOME cases.

74. For restructuring a data base, partitioning WILL/WILL NOT save resources.

75. Encoding of data COSTS/MAY COST/SAVES/MAY SAVE I/O.

76. When encoding is done, that data stored in the data base is ______________ of a larger value.

77. When encoding causes two tables to be physically accessed, then encoding costs I/O. (T/F)

78. When encoding is done so that tables do not have to be dynamically scanned, then encoding ______________ I/O.

79. The decision to encode must be based on all the design factors, such as ______________.

CHAPTER 6

High Availability

This chapter discusses the problems associated with achieving a high degree of system availability in ORACLE. The issues of online availability center around the number of times the system goes down and the amount of time required to bring the system back online. The two principal activities that occur during data base downtime are recovery and reorganization. Techniques for minimizing these activities are discussed.

IMPORTANCE OF DESIGN

There are two essential facets to the online environment: online performance and online availability. Performance is designed into the transactions and data bases of the system; performance is not tuned into the system after the fact. Availability is likewise designed into the system, primarily into the data bases of the system.

Data base availability is primarily a function of the downtime of the system. Some aspects of availability, such as power supply stability, machine failure, and acts of nature are all beyond the control of the data base designer. Fortunately, most system outages are not caused by uncontrollable factors. Most occur at the application or operational level and in fact are very much influenced by the analyst.

RECOVERY/REORGANIZATION

The two primary reasons for system unavailability are the activities of recovery and reorganization. Recovery occurs when there is a system failure and the data and transactions of the system need to be restored. Recovery is an unscheduled event, unlike data base reorganization, which is scheduled. Whenever recovery or reorganization are occurring, the data base is unavailable for other processing. The strategy for high availability is to minimize the time required for recovery and reorganization.

Phases of Recovery

There are three phases to the recovery process. The first is the discovery of the error. Data base size is seldom a factor in the discovery phase. The second phase is the analysis required to understand why the error occurred and what to do about it. Data base size is very much a factor in this phase of recovery. Large data bases often require many resources for diagnostic analysis.

The smaller the data bases, the faster diagnostics can be run. In fact, large data base size may prevent iterative analysis after a failure. And massive amounts of data often mask pertinent information that otherwise would be obvious, or at least easy to get to. Exaggerating the effect of data base size is the fact that the second phase of recovery analysis is often the lengthiest. Anything that can be done to shorten this phase is beneficial.

The third phase of recovery is the prescriptive phase, in which action is taken as a result of the analysis made in the second phase. Depending on the error and the fix, data base size may play a part in this phase. On occasions a fix can be implemented immediately with no significant data manipulation. In this case, data base size is not a factor. In other cases, where data bases must be manipulated, data base size is a factor.

The three phases of recovery are shown by Figure 25.

To minimize the work done in phase 2 or phase 3 of recovery requires that the units of data on which analysis is being done and on which recovery measures are being taken be minimized. Strictly speaking, the size of the physical unit on which analysis and recovery are done is what needs to be minimized.

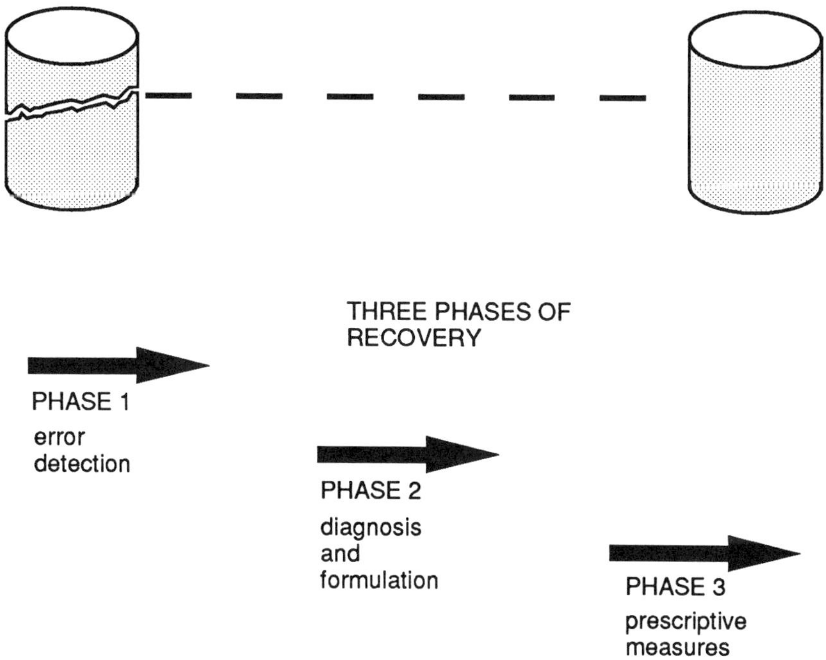

FIGURE 25. Three phases of recovery.

Reorganization—an Unload/Reload Process

Reorganization occurs for many reasons, the most common being the internal disorganization of data at the table and/or at the index level. A reorganization of data has the effect of reconciling the logical and the physical order of data. Disorganized data is physically placed so that the system requires unnecessary I/O to access the data. The degree of organization (or disorganization!) is determined by utilities that monitor the physical placement and access of data.

During a reorganization, data is read in its old state, sorted or modified if necessary, and reloaded in its new state. Once reloaded in its new state, the logical and the physical sequences of the data are synchronized and the system can access the data efficiently. Because of its functional simplicity, a reorganization is sometimes called an unload/reload program.

Figure 26 shows the mechanics of a reorganization.

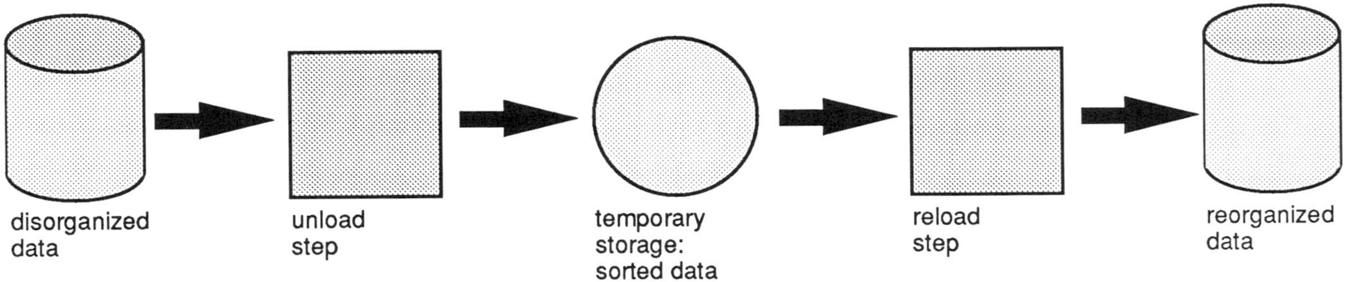

FIGURE 26 The mechanics of data reorganization.

When a table is reorganized its indexes are normally reorganized as well.

But internal disorganization (i.e., unoptimal physical placement of data) is not the only reason for reorganization. When the structure of data undergoes radical redefinition, the data probably needs to be reorganized. The difference between a reorganization for internal data cleanliness and one for radical data redefinition is important. Reorganization for internal cleanliness may be done for (and may actually affect) relatively few rows of data. But reorganization for structure redefinition is done because of a need to modify every row.

The smaller the data base (down to a point!), the faster the recovery and reorganization. The faster recovery and reorganization can be done, the higher the system availability.

Estimating Downtime

The analyst knows a data base is too large by estimating the time required for recovery and reorganization. To estimate the time needed for the execution of these utilities, the size of the data base must be estimated by calculating the amount of data in the row, the overhead in the row, the number of rows, the freespace in the page and the number of free pages, and the space required for an index.

All indexes should be taken into account, and levels of index space must be factored in. In addition, data base size as the data base goes into full production must be estimated, not just the size of the data base immediately after implementation.

After the size of the data base is estimated, recovery and reorganization time must be calculated. There are several approaches to this calculation. One approach is to compare the recovery needs with a similar table that is already in existence. As long as there is the same number of indexes and as long as row size and the number of occurrences of rows are approximately the same, the comparison is valid, at least in gross terms.

Another approach is to prototype the recovery and reorganization needs. Usually, a small amount of data is used in the prototype and an extrapolation is done. If there is any question as to the recovery and reorganization requirements for a data base, a prototype should be done.

Generally speaking, a prototype is done using either 10 percent of the data that will actually exist or, for large data bases, one spindle's worth of data. In addition, the prototype must include one occurrence of each foreign key relationship that will exist. Another consideration is the representative population of tables, especially tables that are often accessed and have multiple foreign keys.

One factor that cannot be prototyped is the phase 2 recovery time—the time spent in analysis. The time estimations for phase 2 must be added to the estimated or prototyped recovery time—which is really phase-3 time.

Probability of Downtime

After the estimates for downtime are created, the probability of downtime must be calculated. Generally speaking, the downtime pattern of a shop is constant—some shops experience very few outages and other shops experience frequent outages. The frequency of outages is due to several factors: design, implementation, operations, etc. The track record of a shop should be the guiding factor in the estimation of the frequency of outages. As a result, it does not matter whether the probability of outage is being calculated for a new system or the rewrite or enhancement of an older system.

The probability of an outage should be considered along with the length of the outage to determine if system availability goals will be met. It is assumed that availability goals have been established in a formal, quantified manner. If system availability goals have not been established, then there can be no objective measurement against the goals.

Reducing the Volume of Data

The following analysis should be done for every data base that is large and requires a significant amount of uptime.

To reduce the volume of data, the first (very basic) question to be asked is whether all the data is necessary and whether the data will be used. Figure 27 shows a data base in which only a small portion of the data base will ever be accessed.

In Figure 27, only a portion of the data will ever be accessed, but the data that will not be accessed is still expensive to maintain in an automated form.

Analysis should be done to determine what data can be culled from the data base. Typical criteria for culling data include the age of the data, the size of the account that is being represented, the size of the customer whose data is kept, active data versus inactive data, and so forth. There are probably an infinite number of criteria for the culling of data. Each criterion serves to separate the data with a high probability of access from the data with a low probability of access.

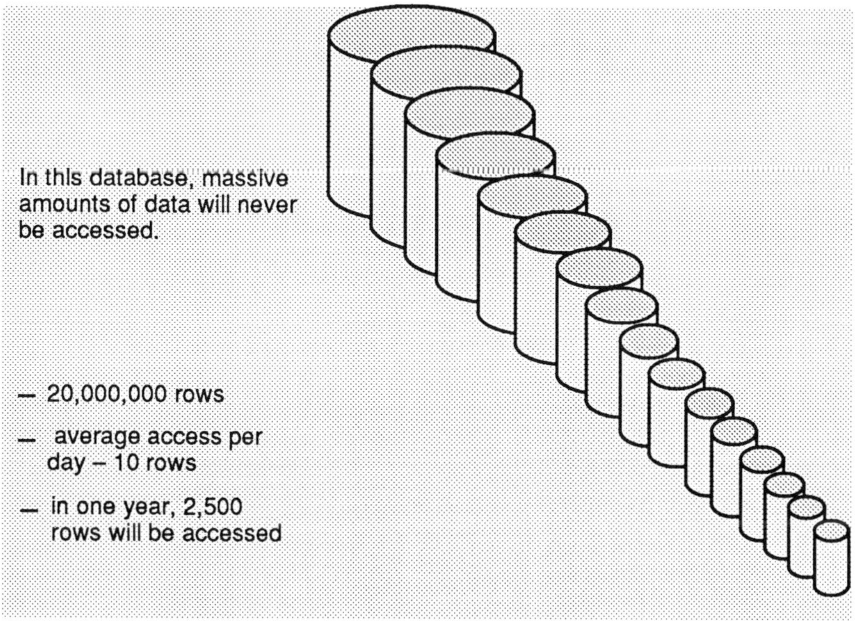

FIGURE 27. In this data base, massive amounts of data will never be accessed.

If there are large volumes of data that will never or very infrequently be accessed, then clearly some reduction of data is in order.

On occasion, the system requirements will specify that data is needed but that only very infrequently will some of the data be accessed. At this point, the economics of user requirements enter the picture. What is the cost of storing and maintaining data online when it will seldom be needed?

Most likely, a more cost-effective alternative is to store the data offline, on magnetic tape or other medium. Offline storage does not mean that the data cannot be accessed, but that access to the data will be slower than online access. The separate costs of offline storage and offline access are much lower than the corresponding online costs, however.

The utility of faster access and slower access must be measured against the associated costs.

The first level of availability analysis questions whether the data is cost justified in the first place. The second level follows directly from the first. Has there been a conscious and deliberate split of primitive and derived data? (For an in-depth discussion of primitive and derived data, refer to *Information Engineering for the Practitioner*, Yourdon Press, 1987, or to *Data Architecture: The Information Paradigm*, QED, 1989.)

Generally speaking, primitive data is stored online and derived data is moved offline or closer to the end user community. One criterion to determine whether data is primitive or derived is that primitive data is vulnerable to update and derived data is not. This criterion fits very nicely with the movement of derived data to offline storage and processing.

The third level of analysis calls for the split of administrative and operational data. This split does not reduce data base size. Instead it ensures that data is as untangled as possible. Operational data is data directly concerned with the day-to-day operations of the enterprise. Administrative data is that related to the administration of the enterprise. For example, in a banking environment, customer and account data are operational; employee payroll, insurance processing, and salary administration data are administrative.

The splitting of administrative and operational data does not imply that either one should be online (as was the implication of the split of primitive and derived data). Instead the separation allows the data and the accompanying processes to be moved to separate systems if need be, or the recovery or reorganization of one set of data independent of the other. A failure in the operational world will have no effect on the administrative world, and vice versa.

The fourth level of analysis calls for the separation and segregation of one application from the next. Unlike the split between administrative and operational data, the split of applications into their own distinct units is not easily accomplished after the system has been designed. If this split is to be done, it is most effective prior to the building of actual data bases.

However, like the split of operational and administrative data, no data is purged from the online environment. Data is separated into small units so that recovery and reorganization can be done quickly and independently on each unit. The failure of one unit has no effect on other units, further enhancing the availability posture.

The fifth level of analysis occurs for single applications that are large and that still have an availability exposure. For a single application, consideration must be given to the splitting of the application according to the key values of the data bases. The total amount of data is not reduced; instead, the data is spread over distinct units, each of which is smaller than the collective data base.

There is a good way to reduce the unit of recoverability in ORACLE. When data is split within the application there are separate tables that are defined to ORACLE. Each table contains the same type of data, but data with a different key value. For example, one table contains all keys whose values are from A to H. Another table contains all keys whose values are from I to P. And a third table contains values whose keys begin with Q to Z. Such a split can be termed creating "like" partitions. Then one table is defined to one instance of ORACLE, another table is defined to another instance of ORACLE, and so forth. In such a fashion, the workload can be split over multiple instances of ORACLE without altering the application significantly.

Figure 28 illustrates the split of data.

One disadvantage of building like partitions is that ORACLE is totally unaware of the relationship between any two partitions. In the eventuality that *all* of the like partitions need to be recovered or reorganized, ORACLE will not be aware of any need for coordination.

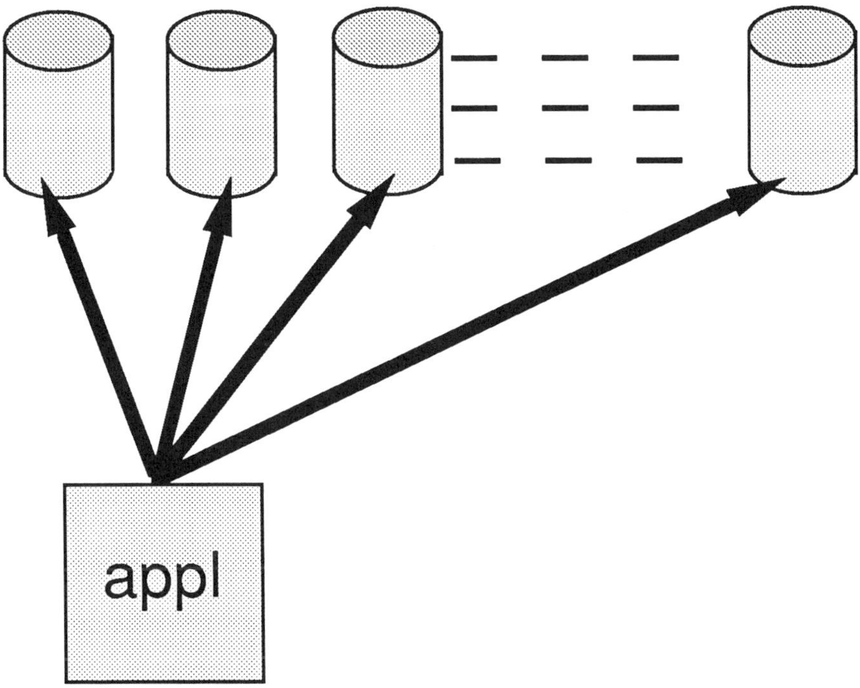

FIGURE 28. Splitting data at the application level into "like" partitions.

A major advantage of like partitions of data is that each like data base can be reorganized and recovered independently. The unit of reorganization and recovery has been reduced to a minimum.

Splitting data across an application using like partitions has many ramifications, each of which must be considered by the analyst. One consideration is the interface with other applications. If one application has a key split by line of business and another application has a key split by marketing division, then interfacing the two systems may be complex. Furthermore, splitting both of them onto separate processors may prove difficult if there is any amount of interaction at all between the systems.

A second consideration of splitting data is in the effectiveness of the split. If a data base is split into 10 like partitions, but 90 percent of the data resides in a single partition, then the split has not been effective. Figure 29 shows such an occurrence.

Also, the analyst must consider not just today's data and distribution of data but tomorrow's trends as well.

One of the significant advantages of splitting data at the application level is that the impact of failure is limited. Not only does recovery occur more quickly, but the data that is impacted by the failure is significantly less. Consider a large data base that is not split. Suppose the data base experiences a failure. Because of its size, recovery takes a long time and much data is made unavailable as the recovery is effected. Now consider that same data base that has been split into like partitions. The same error occurs and one of the partitions is unavailable. But the other like partitions are up and running. Fur-

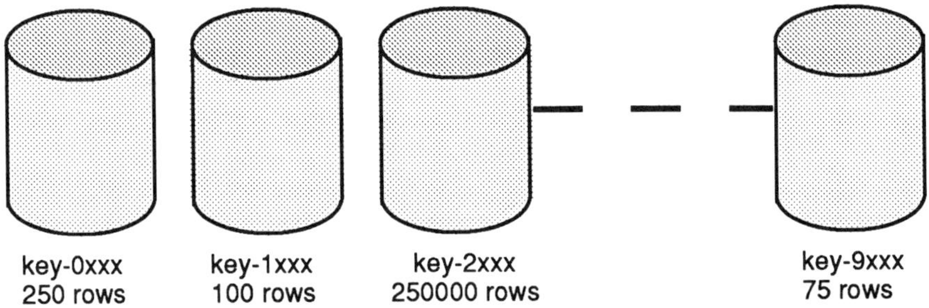

FIGURE 29. Even though the keys have been evenly distributed, the data in the partitions has not been evenly distributed, defeating the purpose of partitioning data into like partitions.

thermore, it takes only a fraction of the time required to repair the large data base to repair the like partition.

SUMMARY

In summary, this chapter has discussed the issues of availability from the perspective of the options that are available to the designer. The reduction of the raw amount of data was the first option considered. Next came the option of separating derived from primitive data, and then the separation of administrative and operational data, as well as the separation of data by application. Finally, the splitting of data bases within the same application was considered, which allows the designer to reduce the data into as fine a unit of recovery and reorganization as desired.

QUESTIONS: HIGH AVAILABILITY

1. There are two factors to availability: the ______________ of time the computer stays down when it goes down, and the ______________ of outages.
2. Before a design can be undertaken, a ______________ goal of availability needs to be set.
3. Two common activities that cause system outages are ______________ and ______________.
4. Reorganization IS/IS NOT a scheduled activity.
5. Recovery IS/IS NOT a scheduled activity.
6. The general strategy to minimize the length of time required for recovery or reorganization is to ______________ minimize the amount of data in a data base.
7. A reorganization is often called an ______________ process.
8. There are ______________ phases to recovery.
9. The first phase of recovery is the ______________ of an error.
10. The first phase of recovery IS/IS NOT sensitive to data base size.
11. The second phase of recovery is the ______________ phase.
12. In the diagnostic phase, the reason the error occurred is addressed. (T/F)
13. In the second part of the diagnostic phase, a plan is ______________ for correcting the error.
14. Data base size IS/IS NOT a factor in the second phase of recovery.

15. Large data bases often hide relevant diagnostic information. (T/F)
16. Diagnostics usually require more time to execute in the face of ______________ data bases.
17. The third phase of recovery is the ______________ phase.
18. The prescriptive phase IS/IS NOT sensitive to data base size.
19. Which two phases of recovery are sensitive to data base size?
20. Which two phases of recovery usually take the most time?
21. Which phases of recovery require an indeterminate number of resources?
22. Reorganization of data is done to reorder the ______________ structure of data and to ______________ data when the entire data structure needs to be changed.
23. The time required for reorganization is directly proportional to the amount of data to be reorganized. (T/F)
24. The number of indexes to be reorganizedf IS/IS NOT of minor importance.
25. Comparing data bases of equivalent ______________ and ______________ is a good way to estimate downtime needs.
26. Estimation of data base size includes ______________.
27. All ______________ of indexes must be established in calculating data base size.
28. Variable-length fields—in order to estimate space—need to be estimated at their MINIMUM/AVERAGE/MAXIMUM space required.
29. Data base size at full maturity is the ______________ goal for the estimation target.
30. If comparisons to existing data bases cannot be made in order to estimate downtime, another approach is to ______________ data.
31. The results of an estimation or a prototype should be shielded from the user, especially if the results show the user's downtime needs will not be met. (T/F)
32. After the length of recovery time is estimated, the ______________ of downtime must likewise be estimated.
33. A shop's past ______________ is a good indicator of the probability of an outage.
34. The first analytical step taken to reduce the amount of data to be

recovered is to question whether all the data that will be stored online is ____________.

35. Online storage of data is ____________.

36. Online storage of data that will never be used is especially ____________.

37. Offline storage of data MEANS/DOES NOT MEAN that data cannot be accessed.

38. Offline access and storage of data is less ____________ than online storage and access of data.

39. Offline access of data is SLOWER/FASTER/ABOUT THE SAME as online access of data.

40. ____________ data is usually stored online; ____________ data is stored in a medium convenient to the end user.

41. When primitive data is mixed with derived data, the result is the storage of ____________ amounts of data.

42. Operational data should be separated from ____________ data.

43. When operational data and administrative data are separated, there IS/IS NOT a net loss of data.

44. The segregation of administrative data and operational data has the effect of breaking data into small, finely separated groups. (T/F)

45. Separating unlike ____________ has the same effect as segregating administrative data and operational data.

46. The final option to reduce data base size is to separate data at the ____________ level.

47. Key splits MUST/MAY BE/OUGHT TO BE designed into the application at the moment of inception of the design.

48. Key splits allow applications to run on separate ____________.

49. If a key split can be done once, generally it can be done ____________ times.

50. In ORACLE, data can be split at the ____________ level.

51. When partitioning of data is done, a reorganization for the purpose of restructuring data can be done for individual partitions. (T/F)

52. When partitioning of data is done, a reorganization for the purpose of physically reordering a data base can be done ____________ of other partitions.

53. When partitioning is done by the application, ORACLE knows which partitions need to be recovered. (T/F)
54. When data is split at the application level, processing MAY/MAY NOT be split over more than one processor.
55. When data is split at the application level, ORACLE WILL/WILL NOT know about the relationship among different, logically related data bases.

CHAPTER 7

ORACLE Transaction Design

The first step in the achievement of consistent online performance in ORACLE production applications is the establishment of the appropriate environment. The next step is the proper design of applications. Application design for performance has two components: data base design and transaction design. Data base design, discussed earlier, centers around arranging data so that a minimum of physical I/O is required in its access and update. Transaction design—an equal partner to data base design in the achievement of consistently good application performance—is discussed in this chapter.

ORACLE PERFORMANCE IN THE FACE OF "UNDESIGNED" TRANSACTIONS

A "designed" transaction is one that is constructed in a disciplined manner in order to:

- Achieve the user's function
- Use a minimal amount of resources

To build and maintain adequate ORACLE online performance, all transactions running during the peak online period must be "designed."

The importance of designed transactions being mixed in the online workload with undesigned transactions is best illustrated by an example. Suppose a designed transaction, which uses a minimal amount of resources (i.e., I/Os), is represented by a small box or rectangle, analogically representing the usage of a small number of resources. Suppose an undesigned transaction, which uses an indeterminate number of resources—either large or small—is represented analogically by a large box or rectangle, which suggests the consumption of many resources. What happens when these two types of activities—designed and undesigned—are mixed in the same system? Figure 30 shows the results.

At 8 A.M., when the system is very lightly loaded and a few designed transactions are flowing through the system, system response time is in the 1- to 2-second range. Note that machine utilization is around 10 to 15 percent in this time zone.

At 9 A.M., the system is fully loaded but is operating only on designed transactions. Response time is in the 4- to 5-second range for all transactions, with machine utilization over 85 percent.

At 10 A.M., the system is at its peak usage. In the queue, waiting to use the system, are many designed transactions. In the processor are several undesigned transactions that are in execution. The system is running at the speed of its slowest activity, which happens to be undesigned transactions. The speed of the undesigned transactions through the system is indeterminate.

Designed transactions that took 2 to 3 seconds at 8 A.M. may take 30 to 45 minutes at 10 A.M. The designed transactions' speed through the system depends on queue time, which has nothing to do with the resources required by the transaction that is queued, but has everything to do with the resources required by the transactions queued in front of the transaction. (Note: the diagram at 10 A.M. is pedagogically designed to show the worst that can happen in online systems.) However, machine utilization is high throughout this period.

At 1 P.M., in a less fully loaded state, the system exhibits a fluctuating set of characteristics. Some of the time, when there are few undesigned transactions in the system, the system yields good response time; at other times, when there are many undesigned transactions in the system, the system yields spotty response time. Note that system utilization varies widely in this configuration.

ORACLE performance, in an unarchitected environment (i.e., where designed and undesigned transactions are freely mixed) is said to fluctuate with the workload. In other words, when the workload has one makeup of transactions, response time is good; when the workload has another makeup of transactions, the response time is bad. The

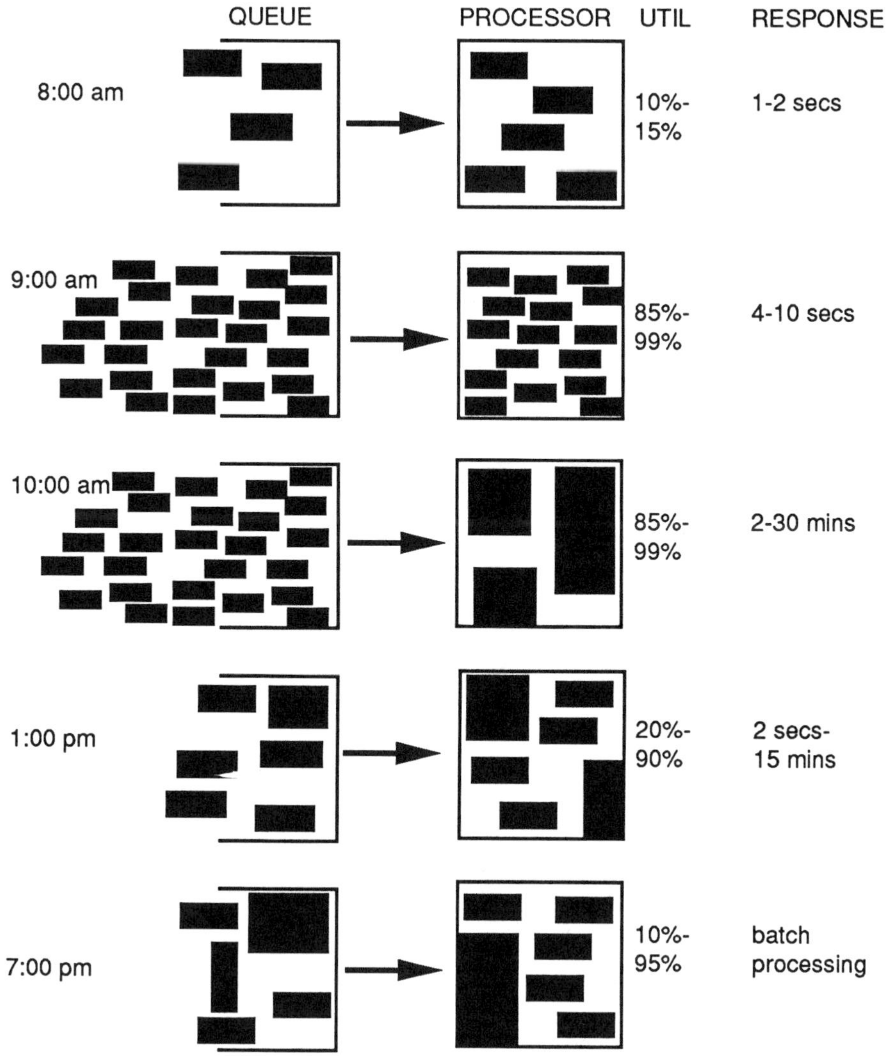

FIGURE 30. The results of mixing designed and undesigned transactions in the same system.

fairly normal state illustrated at 1 P.M. in Figure 30 reinforces this notion.

Finally, in the evening (in the example, around 7 o'clock) the batch processing begins and the ORACLE environment turns into an exclusively batch environment.

Why do ORACLE systems, when fully loaded, exhibit the performance characteristics described by the vignette in Figure 30, and what can be done about it?

Why Undesigned Transactions in ORACLE Damage Online Performance

In ORACLE, undesigned transactions damage overall system performance because of the queue time they can cause for other transactions entering the system or executing after they have gone into execution. In other words, a transaction's largest impediment to overall system performance is the resource utilization of the transactions that are queued in front.

As an illustration of this simple principle, suppose a person wishes to cash a check. At the bank there are two lines, line A and line B, that the person may enter. Both are approximately the same length and both are served by competent tellers who operate at roughly the same speed. Which line, then, should the person enter in order to get the best service?

Suppose in line A everyone wants to either cash a check or change a $10 bill, activities that require only a small amount of time. Suppose in line B everyone except one person wishes to cash a check. That person wishes to balance his or her checkbook and verify every transaction for the last six months with the records of the bank. In this case line B will be much slower than line A because of the nature of the activities of the people in the queue.

This simple bank queuing example illustrates the effect of placing an undesigned transaction in a queue with designed transactions. The designed transactions that are queued behind the undesigned transactions run at the speed of the undesigned transactions, which is slow.

What to Do About Undesigned Transactions

Several options in the management of undesigned transactions are—

1. Recognize undesigned transactions as they enter the system and do not allow them to be queued with designed transactions. This solution makes the assumption that undesigned transactions can be recognized prior to execution and that some queue for the "slow" undesigned transactions exists where they won't be harmful to performance.

The first assumption—that undesigned transactions can be recognized upon entry into the system—is only very partially true. Many transactions must go into execution before the resources used by the transaction are apparent. But by the time the transaction goes into execution, it is too late to protect online resources.

Furthermore, even if there were a way to recognize undesigned transactions, a considerable amount of resources would be required because every transaction, upon entry to the system, must be analyzed to determine whether it is "designed" or "undesigned."

The second assumption is that there is a queue into which to send the undesigned transactions to get them out of the way of the designed transactions. If the undesigned queue is one that runs after-hours, then there is no problem with online performance. Unfortunately, the problem arises because a user submitting an undesigned transaction must wait until the next day to receive the output from his or her request for processing.

But merely assigning all undesigned transactions their own queue, and then letting the queue operate on online data bases in tandem with queues that hold designed transactions, opens up other impediments to performance. Shared buffer pools, disk access of data (i.e., arm and head movement), internal integrity mechanisms and facilities, etc., are all shared by online queues of transactions—whether the queue is designed or not. Consequently, performance exposures abound even when undesigned transactions are removed to their own queue and are allowed to access commonly shared data on the same processor as designed transactions.

2. Allow the system to page undesigned transactions out whenever the system reaches the state portrayed by 10 A.M. in Figure 32. Certainly, when the undesigned transaction is paged out, designed transactions are allowed to flow through the system quickly. But there are some major drawbacks to paging as a solution to performance. The first and most obvious is the resources required for paging.

Paging causes physical I/O just like a regular read or write of a data base. But the problems of paging run deeper. Not all undesigned transactions can be conveniently paged out.

Suppose an undesigned transaction is updating an entire data base and is partially through with the update. To maintain integrity of the data either all of the data base updates must be backed out or all data that has been updated and potentially can be updated must be protected against further access or update until the paged program can be re-entered into the system. In the case where paging occurs and data is left protected, if one of the transactions that wishes to execute needs to go against the data that has been protected, then deadlock occurs and a real performance bottleneck is created. In the case where a massive backout of data base updates occurs, the resource requirements are tremendous. An irony is that once the program is paged back in, the updates must be re-applied once more, using even more resources.

Because of the automatic inefficiencies of paging and the problems of data base update integrity, paging is not a popular option.

3. Have designed and undesigned transactions separated by the end user at the moment of entry into the online system. Another option (that realistically has limited applicability) is to require the end user to separate designed and undesigned transactions prior to the entry into the online system. Surprisingly, when this option is applicable, it is a very plausible solution. Unfortunately, this option is applicable only infrequently. Requiring end users to separate designed transactions from undesigned transactions requires a sophisticated and motivated end user.

Most users lack the background to be able to distinguish an undesigned transaction from a designed transaction. Even when the end user can make this distinction, he or she is hard pressed to say why the separation should be made.

Furthermore, suppressing the submissions of transactions requires a user to sacrifice immediate personal needs for the good of the online community. Most end users do not understand or support such approaches. Consequently, voluntary separation of end user requests based on resource consumption is an infrequently chosen option.

4. Create separate designed and undesigned transactions at the design level and allow only designed transactions to run online in the peak processing period. In the long run, this option is easily the most effective (and, ironically, the most inexpensive).

Furthermore, it is noted that every undesigned transaction can be broken into a series of designed transactions, although at first this transformation capability is not apparent. More important, the notion of transforming undesigned transactions into designed transactions fits very closely with the establishment of the production environment, as has been discussed.

CHARACTERISTICS OF DESIGNED AND UNDESIGNED TRANSACTIONS

The preceding discussion explains why online systems are so sensitive to designed and undesigned transactions. In short, under any volume of processing, ORACLE cannot tolerate undesigned transactions and sustain good online performance.

What are the different characteristics of designed and undesigned transactions in ORACLE? The primary difference between them is the resource consumption of the transaction, and resource consumption revolves primarily around the I/Os consumed.

In general, a designed transaction will consume no more than 8 to 10 physical I/Os per execution of the transaction. An undesigned transaction may consume an indeterminate number of I/Os—from 15 to 15,000 plus.

ORACLE TRANSACTION DESIGN

Data-Driven Processes

A word of caution is in order concerning a special class of transactions. Some undesigned transactions consume a small amount of I/O in some cases, and in other cases, depending upon the data on which they are operating, they consume large amounts of I/O. Such transactions are referred to as "data-driven" processes.

For example, suppose a canned query is made in which a bank teller can query the monthly activity for an account. John Jones queries his account in 4 I/Os; Mary Smith queries her account in 6 I/Os; and the accounts receivable clerk for IBM queries the IBM account in 15,000 I/Os. The amount of resource consumption of any given transaction depends not as much on the efficiency of the calls of the transaction or the optimization of the efficiency of the path of calls, but on the amount of data on which the transactions operate.

The amount of resource consumption of a data-driven transaction depends on the data on which the transaction operates, not on any superficial analysis by a call optimizer. Data-driven transactions are one of the variables that make distinguishing designed transactions from undesigned transactions prior to execution very difficult.

I/Os

I/Os, then, are the primary resource consumed by transactions that separate designed transactions from undesigned transactions. Why is I/O the most critical factor?

I/Os operate at mechanical speeds—in the millisecond range. Other computer operations operate in the electrical range—at nanosecond speeds. Electronic speeds are about two to three orders of magnitude faster than mechanical speeds; consequently, the flow of activities in an online environment is constrained by I/O because of I/O's mechanical nature.

But I/O consumption, as singularly important as it is, is not the only reason why undesigned transactions throttle performance.

Data Contention

Consider the probability of contention for data in the light of undesigned and designed transactions. A designed transaction accesses a limited amount of data. Because it operates on a limited amount of data, the chances are good that the designed transaction will not try to access data that is already locked by another online transaction. Furthermore, the designed transaction will lock up only a small amount of data. And, finally, since the designed transaction executes only a small amount of instructions, it locks up its data for only a short amount of time.

Now consider undesigned transactions, which access much data. The odds are good that they will attempt to access data that is already locked by another transaction. The differences between designed and undesigned transactions are illustrated by Figure 31 and Figure 32.

Since the undesigned transaction runs for a long period of time, the odds are good that the data that is locked will be locked for a long period of time. All of these factors increase the probability of contention for data in the online environment.

The solution to contention is obvious. Simply do not allow undesigned transactions to run during the peak period of processing, when online response time is critical.

TRANSACTION ISSUES

The ORACLE DML—SQL—operates on sets of data, not on records of data. To achieve good performance, the designer must structure the usage of SQL so that only very limited sets of data can be retrieved or operated on.

Some of the techniques for minimizing the resources used by a transaction are:

- Do not use language structures that will require full or partial data base scans such as AVERAGE, SUM, etc.

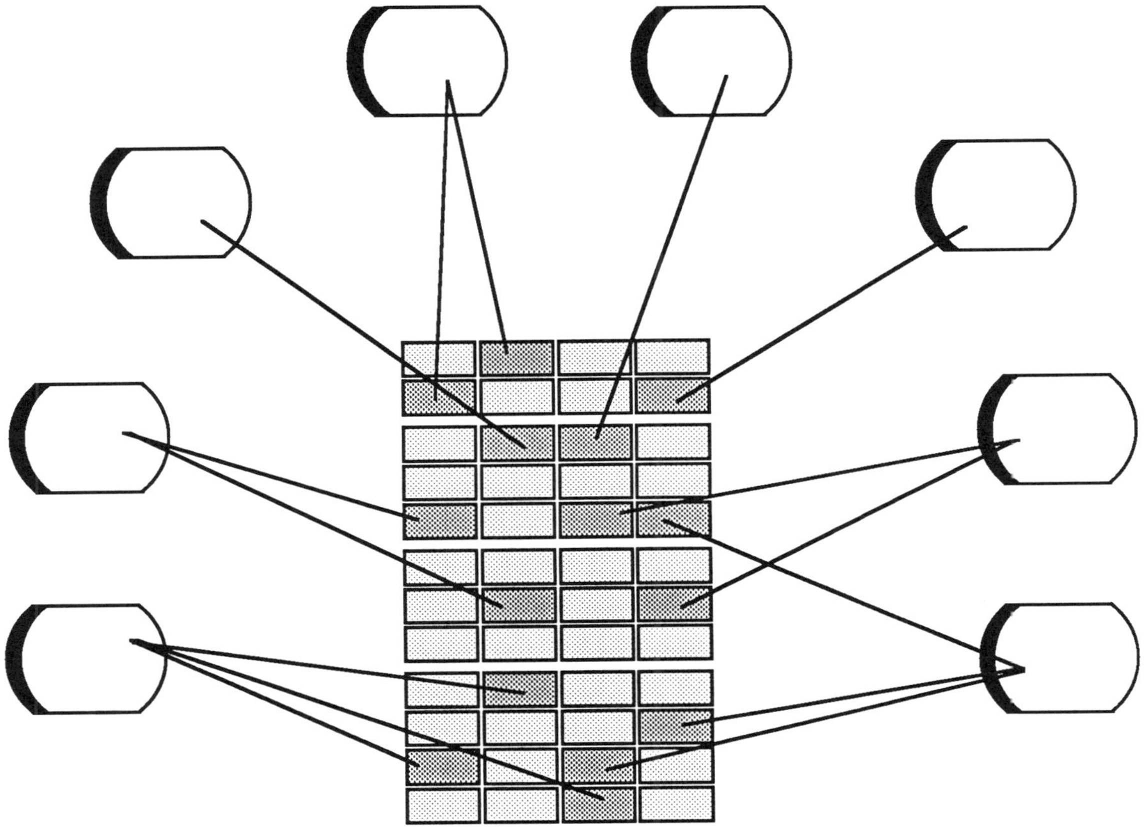

FIGURE 31. When each online user grabs only a small amount of data, the probability of conflict is minimal.

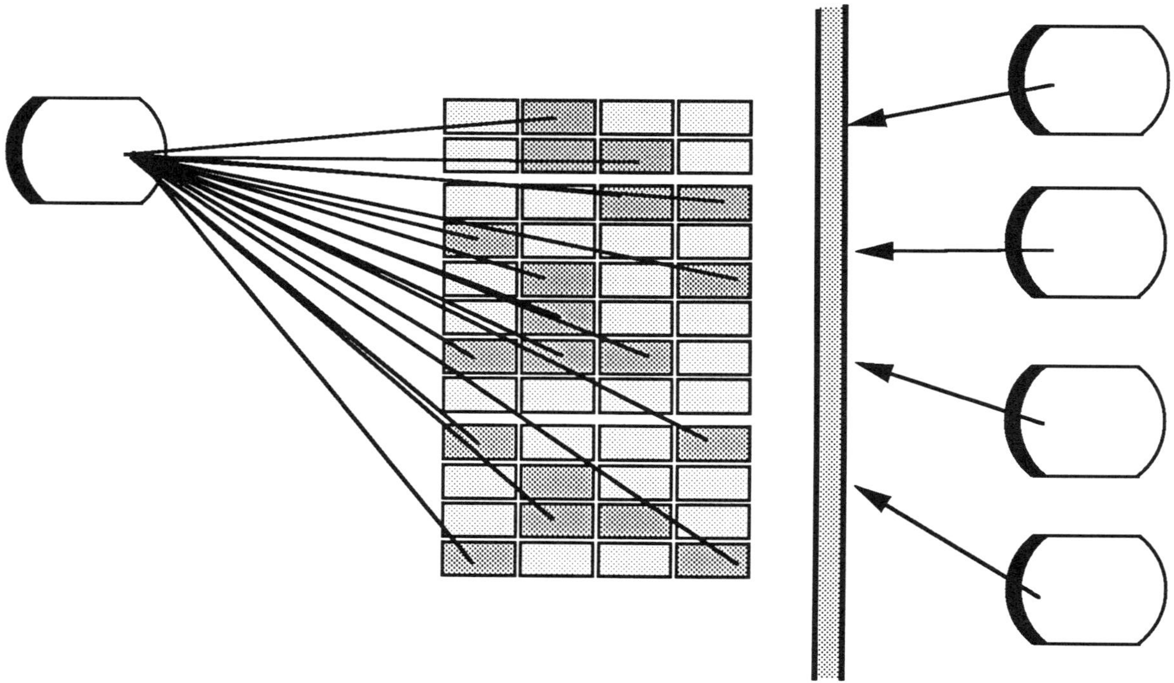

FIGURE 32. When one transaction accesses and locks much data, especially for a lengthy period of time, the probability of conflict is great.

- Do not use search criteria based on nonindexed fields.
- Fully qualify every SQL query so that the absolute minimum of data is accessed. Ideally, one row will satisfy every SQL call.
- When multiple SQL rows are needed, retrieve no more than 10 rows per execution of the transaction.
- When views are used, do not use views that access data across multiple tables.
- When foreign keys must be used to relate data, do not use the foreign key relationships more than 10 times in the execution of the transaction.
- Do not do relational joins during the online peak period of processing.
- Do not do DDL processing during peak-period processing.

EXAMPLES OF DESIGNED AND UNDESIGNED TRANSACTIONS

The following illustrates what a designed transaction looks like and how an undesigned transaction may be transformed into a designed transaction. Consider the access of the simple data base shown in Figure 33.

PART NO	DESCR	U/M	CLASS	QOH
461-J	Mold	unit	p	45
491-A	Bed	unit	p	13
513-L	Casing	unit	p	186
515-Q	Joint	vat	np	50000
521-T	Brace	box	np	106
521-X	V-Brace	box	np	35
---------	---------	-------	------	------

FIGURE 33. PART/INVENTORY table—the primary key is part number, the table is clustered.

An example of a designed transaction might be:

```
SELECT PARTNO QOH DESC
FROM PARTABLE
WHERE PART = "515-q'
```

The result of the transaction is:

```
""515-q, 50000, joint''
```

From a resource utilization perspective the question becomes, What amount of I/O was required to process the simple transaction?

Of course, every transaction has a certain amount of overhead I/O—receiving the query from the terminal and sending results back to the terminal represent I/O that is required for every transaction regardless of any other activities. But this ordinary I/O, as long as it is not excessive, is not of great concern to the system developer. Instead, the system developer addresses the incremental I/O used by a transaction.

In the example, one or more I/O is required to access the index looking for the key—part number 515-q (assuming the index has not been placed entirely in memory, which is not likely for an index for a large production data base). The I/O to the index yields the page number needed, and another I/O is done to find the page that contains the row being sought.

Of course, if by chance the page that was being sought were already in the buffer area, no I/O would be needed. In all, a maximum of two data base I/Os will be required to service the transaction—easily within the bounds of a designed transaction.

As long as all online transactions are within the boundaries of a designed transaction (as far as resource consumption is concerned), ORACLE performance will be optimal.

Contrast the simple designed transaction described above with the following data-driven, undesigned transaction. Using the data base shown in Figure 33 and assuming that there is an index on description, the following SQL request is made:

```
SELECT PARTNO QOH
FROM PARTABLE
WHERE DESC = "NUT'
```

The amount of I/O needed to satisfy this request is indeterminate and potentially large. If there are 500 parts that satisfy the criteria and if 3 index pages must be read, then 503 I/Os will need to be done (discounting a few fortuitous hits in the buffer). If there are 10 parts with a description of "NUT," then 10 I/Os plus at least one I/O for the index will be required.

In short, not until the transaction goes into execution will it be known whether it is going to violate the criteria for being designed or undesigned. But certainly 500 plus I/Os violates the criteria for being a designed transaction. (Note: this transaction is a classical example of a data-driven transaction and illustrates the difficulty of predetermining designed and undesigned transactions prior to execution.)

A third type of transaction is illustrated by the following request:

```
SELECT COUNT(*)
FROM PARTABLE
WHERE CLASS = "P'
```

In this case, the analyst wishes to determine how many parts classified as precious goods (i.e., where class = P) there are in the data base. He or she assumes that no index exists on class because it is a commonly occurring value.

The number of I/Os required is the number of pages there are in the data base. If the data base is large and there are 1500 pages, then 1500 I/Os will be required. Unlike the previously discussed transaction, which, depending on the data, may or may not require much I/O, it is predictable that this will be an undesigned transaction for anything but the smallest of tables.

To achieve good, consistent online performance, none of the undesigned transactions must be allowed to execute during online, peak-period processing.

CREATING DESIGNED TRANSACTIONS

The first question the developer must ask is whether large batch-sequential scans of data should be done during peak-period processing in the first place. Philosophically, what is the business function served by batch-sequential scans and are those scans cost justified? This question must be thoroughly addressed before proceeding. In general, most sequential processing will be relegated to the off-hours processing window.

But if the user absolutely insists on doing large, batch-oriented data base scans online, then at the very least those scans must be repackaged to fit within the requirements of the peak period processing window.

Controlling resource consumption under ORACLE is difficult, but not impossible, because SQL does set-at-a-time processing of data. To illustrate the difficulty of controlling resource utilization under normal SQL, consider the following simple SQL program operating against the table found in Figure 33.

```
SELECT PARTNO
FROM PARTABLE
WHERE CLASS = "P' AND PARTNO < "1000'
```

Such a SQL statement would effectively retrieve only parts with a key less than 1000 where class equals P and, probably depending on the data base, use a modest amount of I/O, however ORACLE chose to access the data. Of course, the number of parts retrieved depends upon knowledge of the data base. If there are few parts from a key range of 0000 to 1000, then the query will use few resources. If there are many parts between 0000 and 1000, then the selection criteria can be narrowed down to a smaller range, say from 000 to 100. Of course, intelligent range selection of this type depends on the data being indexed and clustered by part number.

But the program would be a strange one indeed because many other parts undoubtedly exist that satisfy the criteria beyond the key range selected.

In keeping with using a small amount of resources for each online execution, if the user wishes to continue to scan the data, then he or she can remember where the last part number was that was accessed, go to that part, and sequentially scan some more parts.

Suppose part 1258-QX was the last part retrieved. The following SQL program can then be used to continue the batch scan:

```
SELECT PARTNO
FROM PARTABLE
WHERE CLASS = "P' AND
PARTNO BETWEEN "01258-QX' AND "02000-ZZ'
```

This process (where the parameters of the set being accessed are reset for every execution) can be iterated for as long as the end user desires, retrieving a small amount of data in each execution of the program and beginning each execution where the previous one left off.

When data is accessed by physical colocation sequence, then many parts may be retrieved per iteration. Fifty or sixty parts may be retrieved for each iteration because less I/O will be required in going from one part to the next.

But there are some pitfalls to the simple approach described here. One is that between executions the data that is being queried may in fact be updated. For example, suppose in iteration *n* the last part number retrieved was 9409-MZ. Immediately after the *n*th execution the part number was deleted by some other transaction. Now, on the *n*th + 1 iteration, when the user tries to position the program to part 9409-MZ, there will be no part for repositioning, potentially disrupting the logic of the program.

The technique described here—that of iterating through a batch-sequential scan—has the advantage of requiring only a limited amount of resources and freezing those resources for only a short time. Unfortunately, effective execution of this technique requires a detailed knowledge of the data that is being operated on.

Thus, the technique of reiterating a large scan of data is able to transform an undesigned transaction into a designed transaction. But there is a certain amount of overhead associated with the technique. ORACLE, like all online software, requires a certain amount of initiation and shutdown processing. Each iteration requires this overhead.

Care must be taken by the end user with the coding techniques used in iterating through a data base scan, because ORACLE may not yield the desired performance in every case. Consider what would happen if the data were not indexed and clustered. Suppose the very simple SQL query is issued:

```
SELECT PARTNO UM
FROM PARTABLE
WHERE CLASS = "P' AND
      UM BETWEEN "TON' AND "YARD'
```

In this case, ORACLE will scan the entire data base for *every* execution of the query regardless of where the parameters of set delineation are set because UM is not indexed.

Another approach is to execute only so many instructions and then automatically require the end user to continue processing in off hours. For example, the (pseudo) SQL program accomplishes this objective, as shown below:

```
SELECT PARTNO
FROM PARTABLE
WHERE PARTNO < "1000'
(issue message to continue
 processing offline if more
 parts are desired)
```

Because sets of data are scanned by ORACLE and because ORACLE has limited facilities for monitoring the resources used, controlling resource utilization of nonindexed, nonclustered data is very difficult. But where the designer knows that there is a large amount of unclustered data with like values to be accessed, he or she can artificially introduce criteria at application level that will force sets of data to be subdivided. As a simple example, consider a personnel data base that has employees classified either as male or female (i.e., the field for SEX contains the values M or F).

Any query against the personnel file using sex as a criterion will result in a large number of rows satisfying the criterion and the entire data base being scanned. But suppose an artificial classification is introduced for an employee (call the artificial field ECLASS for employee class). For the first 50 employees the value of 1 is assigned. For the next 50 employees a value of 2 is assigned, and so forth. Now, assume an index is created on SEX and ECLASS. A query can now be done so that SQL does not yield a huge result and a subset of the data base can be scanned in an iterative fashion:

```
SELECT EMPNAME SEX DOHIRE
FROM EMPTABLE
WHERE SEX = "M' AND ECLASS = 1
```

This query will yield all the men with ECLASS = 1, roughly 25 rows on the average, assuming there are about as many women employees as men employees. To retrieve the next set of men employees, ECLASS = 2 is used as the qualifier, and so forth. In such a fashion an indexed, table can be iteratively accessed without using a damaging amount of I/O. Note that without an index on SEX and ECLASS, the entire data base must be scanned with each iteration, certainly defeating the purpose of managing online resources.

The update of ECLASS is an issue using the above scheme. Because ECLASS is artificial, the accuracy of the data is not terribly important (i.e., individual inserts and deletes, as long as there are not too many of them, do not affect the usefulness of the field ECLASS).

But, on occasion, it will be useful to create a batch program (running during the off-peak hours) that will sequentially scan the data base, resetting ECLASS.

In fact, when the selection is based entirely on unindexed fields the entire data base must be scanned. Breaking large scans into a series of smaller scans is practically impossible.

A variation of this same technique is possible if there is an arbitrary division of data that already exists and is indexed and clustered. For example, suppose EMPLNO is an indexed, clustered field and is unique to every employee. The following query effectively separates employees into manageable subsets of data:

```
SELECT EMPNAME SEX DOHIRE
FROM EMPTABLE
WHERE SEX = "M' AND
        EMPNO BETWEEN 000 AND 100
```

This query can expect to receive about 50 replies and operate on only a subset of the data base. As employee number goes from 1 to 100, and so on, a manageable number of I/Os are consumed for each iteration.

Another approach to controlling the I/O done by a SQL program is to break down function very finely. Suppose the functional specifications are issued for a SQL program, as shown in Figure 34.

Figure 34 shows that the function accomplished by SQL processing has been broken into a series of smaller processes that accomplish the same thing. There are many advantages to the separation of function into small components. The first and most obvious advantage is that performance is greatly enhanced (i.e., all processing during peak period is designed). The resources required by any given program in execution are much less than the resources required by the large conglomeration of requirements taken together.

But there are other advantages as well. In the case of the example in Figure 34 when there is a problem encountered in the middle of the execution of processing, the entire processing that has already occurred must be backed out. But when functions are broken down into fine units of execution, the problems that occur can be resolved without backing out otherwise validly processed data.

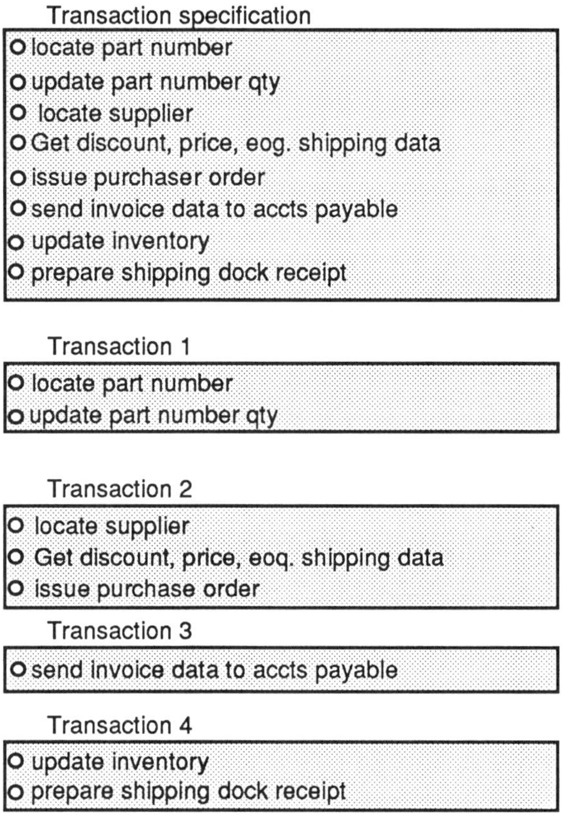

FIGURE 34. Breaking a large function into smaller pieces.

ITERATING A TRANSACTION

In using iterations of transactions, care must be taken to scan a large data base(s) because in some cases iterating transactions can cost I/O and actually hurt performance. Suppose the simple data base, as depicted in Figure 35, is to be scanned.

The data base depicted in Figure 35 is a very large one. A query is to be run against the data base seeking all activities of the amount \$74.32. The first query against the data base looks like:

ACCT	ACT DATE	AMT	LOCATION	ID
0129	860103	12308.90	Fremont	IP
0129	860103	300.00	Fremont	TR
0129	860104	74.32	San Jose	UY
0129	860110	25.00	Sunnyvale	—
------	----------	--------	----------	----
0129	861006	2009.08	Fremont	LK
0129	861008	25.00	Sunnyvale	FL
0129	861019	150.00	Fremont	—
0129	861021	209.00	Santa Cruz	LL
------	----------	--------	----------	----

FIGURE 35. A table indexed, clustered on acct. activity date.

```
SELECT ACCT ACTDATE LOCATION
FROM ACTABLE
WHERE AMT = 74.32 AND
        ACCT BETWEEN 000 AND 100
```

This first query against the data base will access the pages and index for all accounts between 000 and 100—in all, the activity of at most 100 accounts. Depending upon the density and population of the activities and the accounts (i.e., how many activities per account there are and how many accounts there are), a modest amount of I/O will be used. (Note: if the data base being accessed is not indexed, the same data will be retrieved over and over again by each iteration, using a great deal of resources.)

Now, consider the I/O required for the *n*th iteration of the scan (for the purpose of this example $m = n + 1$).

```
SELECT ACCT ACTDATE LOCATION
FROM ACTABLE
WHERE AMT = 74.32 AND
        ACCT BETWEEN n00 AND m00
```

The number of pages to be accessed is the same as in the first iteration, but each iteration causes ORACLE to rescan the index. The amount of I/O used to scan the index mounts up in the face of a very large data base. For small data bases and indexes, this rescanning of the index for each iteration of the transaction presents no problem. But for large amounts of data, this is not the case.

The rescanning of the index for each transaction in the data base for iterative processing points out one of the difficulties of managing large data bases in ORACLE. Of course, the data base could be broken into a series of smaller data bases and many of the performance problems would be minimized.

In the example shown, only the index had to be rescanned for each iteration of the transaction. Suppose the designer had used a selection criteria such that the index was not used by ORACLE. In this case, the entire data base (i.e., the pages) would have to be rescanned from the start for every iteration of the query.

SUMMARY

The second major issue of design for performance is that of transaction design. Transaction design calls for the creation of "designed" transactions, which are those that use a limited amount of resources. Only designed transactions will be allowed to run in the online production environment. The essence of designed transactions is to break large amounts of function into smaller subsets, or to execute long-running transactions in a series of small iterations.

One of the difficulties of ORACLE transaction performance is that SQL operates only on sets of records at one time. To achieve good performance, the sets of records must be broken into subsets.

QUESTIONS: ORACLE TRANSACTION DESIGN

1. The first step in the achievement of online performance in the ORACLE environment is the proper ______________ of the environment.
2. Transaction design and data base design ARE/ARE NOT important if the online environment has not been properly established.
3. After the online environment has been established, BOTH/EITHER transaction design and/or data base design must be done.

4. A "designed" transaction MODIFIES/DOES NOT MODIFY user functionality.
5. A "designed" transaction may cause user function to be repackaged. (T/F)
6. Designed and undesigned transactions SHOULD/SHOULD NOT be mixed during the online day.
7. Undesigned transactions
   a. will never be allowed to run during peak hours
   b. may be allowed
   c. are allowed
8. When transactions arrive faster than the computer can execute them, the ______________ condition has been reached.
9. When the enqueue condition has been reached, response time is a function of two things: how long the transaction takes to execute, and how long the transaction is ______________.
10. When a transaction has reached the enqueue condition, queue time is often much LONGER/SHORTER than execution time.
11. Whether a transaction is designed or not depends on the resources used by the transaction. In general, resources used are measured in terms of
    a. seconds
    b. I/Os
    c. enqueue time
    d. number of instructions
12. I/Os are usually the bottleneck because they operate at mechanical speeds and computers operate at ______________ speeds.
13. The speed of I/O is measured in ______________ seconds.
14. Electronic speeds are measured in ______________ seconds.
15. The I/Os a transaction consumes are directly related to the data base calls done by the transaction. (T/F)
16. The batch window IS/IS NOT sensitive to the running or separation of designed and undesigned transactions.
17. The interactive environment IS/IS NOT sensitive to the running or separation of designed and undesigned transactions.
18. The online environment IS/IS NOT sensitive to the running or separation of designed and undesigned transactions.
19. If designed and undesigned transactions are separated before entry

into the online environment, then performance will not suffer. But separation prior to execution implies that the difference between designed and undesigned transactions can be ______________ ______________.

20. Once a transaction goes into execution, it is too ______________ to recognize that it is undesigned.

21. Even if designed and undesigned transactions can be separated prior to entry into the system, something must be done with undesigned transactions. One solution is to hold the undesigned transactions for processing in the ______________ window.

22. But holding undesigned transactions for the batch window implies overnight turnaround. Overnight turnaround is very user FRIENDLY/UNFRIENDLY.

23. Another alternative is to enter undesigned transactions in a separate queue and run them during the day time. But separate queues running on the same computer still share resources such as ______________.

24. A special kind of undesigned transaction is the ______________ driven process.

25. A data-driven process is one whose resource consumption depends on the data on which it ______________.

26. It is
    a. impossible
    b. very, very difficult
    c. difficult
    d. no problem

    to predetermine how many resources a data-driven process will use.

27. The overhead of predetermining how many resources a data-driven process will use is ______________.

28. ORACLE does set processing. As long as the sets processed are small, then ORACLE transactions can be ______________.

29. When ORACLE processes against large or indeterminate sets, transactions are ______________.

30. The general strategy for ORACLE transactions is to operate against sets of ______________ size.

31. Every undesigned transaction can be broken into a series of designed transactions. (T/F)

32. One way to reduce the resources consumed by an undesigned transaction is to break the ______________ of the undesigned transactions into multiple, small steps.

33. If an undesigned transaction has only one function, another way to break the transaction into pieces is to ______________ the transaction.

34. In addition to breaking up designed transactions, proper coding technique should be used. The following is a list of coding techniques that can be used in the online ORACLE environment: AVERAGE, SUM, ORDER BY. (T/F)

35. Search criteria should be used for indexed fields for online processing. (T/F)

36. All SQL calls should be as fully qualified as possible for online processing. (T/F)

37. No more than 10 rows per iteration of a transaction should be retrieved for online processing. (T/F)

38. Views may span multiple tables for online processing. (T/F)

39. Foreign keys can relate many tables together for many rows for online processing. (T/F)

40. Relational joins are not done during the online day for online processing. (T/F)

41. DDL processing is done only during the batch window. (T/F)

42. Only data base I/O needs to be considered for online processing. (T/F)

43. Data base and index I/O are the primary types of I/O to be considered for online processing. (T/F)

CHAPTER 8

The ORACLE Batch Environment

The first consideration of the production environment is online performance and availability. When adequate online performance cannot be achieved, the question must be asked, Why do transaction processing at all?

But there is more to the production environment than the online peak-period processing. There is the batch environment, which typically occurs during off-peak-period processing hours. The batch environment, then, is that environment in which large sequential processing can be done with no interference with the online, high-performance environment. Even though the ORACLE set processing orientation is ideal for batch sequential processing, there are several aspects to the batch environment that must be carefully considered.

THE BATCH WINDOW

The peak-period processing time frame usually defines—by default—the batch window. That is, everything that is not peak-period is considered to be the batch window, which is thus that period of time when system resources can be used with no impact on online performance. Typically, long sequential processes are run in the batch window.

It is very important that:

- The batch window be carefully estimated.
- The batch window time frame be formally defined.

As long as a shop handles a small amount of processing and/or a small amount of data, then the batch window will probably remain adequate for all the batch needs for the foreseeable future. But in the face of large amounts of processing and/or large amounts of data (as is common in the production environment), the batch window, on occasion, may not be adequate—over time, it tends to shrink. And when the batch window becomes inadequate, the computer operator is left with Hobson's choice: Either run the online environment in a performance-impaired state, or do not do some amount of batch processing. In either case, the end user suffers. When the production environment is being planned, therefore, the batch window should be paid more than casual attention.

To determine if all batch processing will fit in the window, a series of basic measurements can be made. The following example illustrates one of these basic measurements.

Suppose a large data base must be accessed, and suppose there are 10,000 pages of data in the data base. Assume that the index will not be used and that the data is reasonably well organized.

Also assume that no other program will attempt to access the data while access of the data base is occurring. To calculate the length of the batch run, two times are calculated: initiation/shutdown time and data base processing time. (Note that machine time, not elapsed time, is being calculated here.)

$$\text{Processing time} = \text{initiation/shutdown} + \text{data base processing.}$$

Now data base processing time must be calculated. In general, each page of data will require around 25 milliseconds for the I/O needed. (For a processor with a known I/O time larger than 25 milliseconds, adjust the calculation accordingly.)

$$\begin{aligned}\text{Data base processing} &= 10{,}000 \text{ pages} \times 25/1000 \text{ seconds} \\ &= 250 \text{ seconds}\end{aligned}$$

Now assume that 30 seconds of startup/shutdown time is required.

$$\begin{aligned}\text{Processing time} &= 30 \text{ seconds} + (10{,}000 \times 25/1000)\\ &= 280 \text{ seconds}\\ &= 4.66 \text{ minutes of machine time required}\end{aligned}$$

There are many factors other than just the machine requirements that must be considered in the calculation of total batch resources required, however:

- Does the data base have to be scanned sequentially? If it can be scanned in parallel rather than sequentially, then elapsed time may be substantially less than machine time.
- How busy is the machine? Does the machine have to process a heavy workload, and consequently stretch elapsed time significantly longer than the machine time that has been estimated?
- What contention will there be for data? If there is a fair amount of contention for data, elapsed time may be significantly longer than machine time.

In short, the simple calculation presented for machine time requirements gives only a relative figure for the rough estimation of the required length of the batch window.

What Runs In The Batch Window

The kinds of activities that typically run in the batch window include:

- Utilities—back-up, image copies, space management, data analysis, reorganization of data, data definition, etc.
- Application—resorting, merging, summarization, extraction, etc.
- System software—testing, release preparation, etc.

All of the processing requirements for the batch window must be factored into total batch window requirements, but many of the processes that are run are only incidental to the application designer. For example, the designer has very little influence over the data analysis utilities that are run by data administration and data base administration. However, he or she does have influence over such activities as the batch application processing that occurs and the size of the data bases. This chapter will focus on those aspects that can be controlled by the application designer.

I/O AND JOINED DATA BASES

It has been noted that in the online environment data bases that require joins use much I/O and in doing so potentially harm performance. But joined data bases can be detrimental to the amount of resources used in the batch window as well as in the online environment. Careless or uninformed usage of joined data bases can cause massive amounts of I/O to be consumed. The tremendous savings of I/O possible is illustrated by the following example.

Consider the data structure found in Figure 36, in which there are three data bases: a parts data base, a supplier data base, and a parts/supplier cross-reference data base. The intent of processing for the batch program being considered is to create records for each part/supplier relationship for the two data bases—a classical batch-sequential processing activity.

A simple approach is to use a relational join of the two data bases to be scanned and simply create the intersection of the two of them. The relational join would begin with the parts data base and select a part. Next the cross-reference data base would be accessed based upon the value of the part, selecting all the suppliers that supply the part. Then the different suppliers would be accessed, completing the join.

This simple programming technique suggested creates a call pattern as shown by Figure 37.

Figure 37 shows that the parts data base is accessed sequentially, and that the pattern of access suggested above is followed.

The amount of I/O used to process the simple algorithm is considerable. Indeed, just how much I/O is consumed?

The parts data base is scanned sequentially using 250 I/Os (assuming buffer flushing does not occur). The parts supplier data base is likewise scanned sequentially using another 200 I/Os (and likewise assuming buffers are not being rapidly flushed). Then each entry into the supplier data base goes into a different page (except for the occasional fortuitous buffer hit) using 30,000 I/Os. (For the sake of argument, assume 27,000 actual I/Os are done—at a rate of 10 percent fortuitous buffer hits). The number of I/Os needed to process the simple batch join is:

$$250 + 200 + 27{,}000 = 27{,}450 \text{ I/Os}$$

Now consider a much more complex programming approach. Assume that the part/supplier relationship is sorted and is ordered by supplier order. Next the sorted part/supplier data is passed against the supplier

PART	DESCR	U/M	QOH
02158-QX	Ball Bearing	box	900
02158-QZ	Plate	unit	89
01260	Assem 18	crate	125
01268	Assem 980	unit	0
----------	----------	------	---

PART/SUPP XREF	
01258	JONE
01258	KANS
01258	EMPO
01258	JONE
--------	--------

SUPPLIER	NAME	PHONE
Jones Hardware	JP Carson	998-0091
Kansas Supply	JB Riviera	887-4456
Emporium	R D'Field	887-8892
Wilson Supply	B Hackett	998-0023
-----------	-----------	-------------

some database statistics-

Part Table	40 rows/page	250 pages	10000 parts
Part/Supp xref	150 rows/page	300 pages	30000 xref's
Supplier table	25 rows/page	40 pages	1000 supp

FIGURE 36. Some data base statistics.

data base, creating a PART/SUPP/SUPPLIER intermediate record. Now the PART/SUPP/SUPPLIER intermediate records are sorted by part number. Then the parts data base is scanned and matched against the PART/SUPP/SUPPLIER intermediate record, creating the desired part/supplier joined data.

Consider the I/O required to support this algorithm:

1. Sort PART/SUPP into supplier order—200 reads, 200 writes, sort I/O.

Call sequence to join the two databases –

get part 1	get part 1/ suppa	xref	get suppA
	get part 1/ suppG	xref	get suppG
	get part 1/suppL	xref	get suppL
get part 2	get part2/suppB	xref	get suppB
	get part2/suppC	xref	get suppC
	get part2/suppG	xref	get suppG
	get part2/suppM	xref	get suppM
	get part2/suppP	xref	get suppP
get part 3	get part3/suppA	xref	get suppA
get part 4	get part4/suppC	xref	get suppC
	get part4/suppK	xref	get suppK
	get part4/suppL	xref	get suppL
----------	-------------------	-----	------------

FIGURE 37. Call sequence required to join the two data bases using the xref table.

2. Creation of PART/SUPP/SUPPLIER intermediate records—200 reads (part/supply sorted data), 40 reads (suppler data), 200 writes (of the intermediate record, assuming the intermediate record fits into the same number of pages as read out of).
3. Sort intermediate records by part number—200 reads, 200 writes, sort I/O.
4. Merging of intermediate record with parts data—250 reads, 200 reads, 400 writes (assuming the joined record created is long enough to require more space).

The I/O required is, then

step 1	- 400 I/Os	sort I/Os
step 2	- 440 I/Os	
step 3	- 400 I/Os	sort I/Os
step 4	- 850 I/Os	
total	2090 I/Os	2 sort I/Os

Even if the sorts require as much as 1000 I/Os (which is likely a high number), the economics of not using the simple relational join greatly favor a less straightforward approach of sorting and merging data.

The order of magnitude of difference in I/Os used is anything but farfetched. And the I/Os consumed in the batch environment are as important as the I/Os in the online environment when considered collectively for the batch window.

Furthermore, the example shown is for relatively small amounts of data over very simple relationships that use indexed data—i.e., the best of all possible worlds. In something less than the best of all possible worlds, it is safe to say that the I/O consumed by the first approach would be substantially more.

Consequently, the designer must be very careful in the design and management of joined relationships in the batch environment.

PARALLEL SEQUENTIAL RUNS

An important design strategy in the management of the batch window is the ability to break long batch processes into a series of shorter-running processes that can be run in parallel, either on the same machine or on separate machines. Consider the two types of runs shown in Figure 38.

In Figure 38, there are two scenarios. In one all parts are updated in a single batch run, requiring four hours of processing. In the other each batch run updates one-quarter of the data base (i.e., a separate part of the same data base), and an elapsed time of one hour is required. While the same amount of machine resources is required in both scenarios, the elapsed time is much smaller when the batch runs can be broken up and run in parallel.

The ability to break large batch runs into multiple, asynchronously executable shorter batch runs depends upon many factors, such as:

- The ability to insulate data. If all four shorter runs operated on the same data, there would be no point in breaking up the runs.
- The ability of the host processor to multiprocess. If only one task can be run at a time, there is no point in breaking up long batch runs into shorter ones. Often the ability to multiprocess is not a function of the operating system but of the application. Because of the contention for data and the need to run a job serially, classical multiprocessing at the operating system level is not applicable.

The design option that greatly facilitates these goals is the physical separation of data at the application level. When the application divides the data over four physically separate data bases:

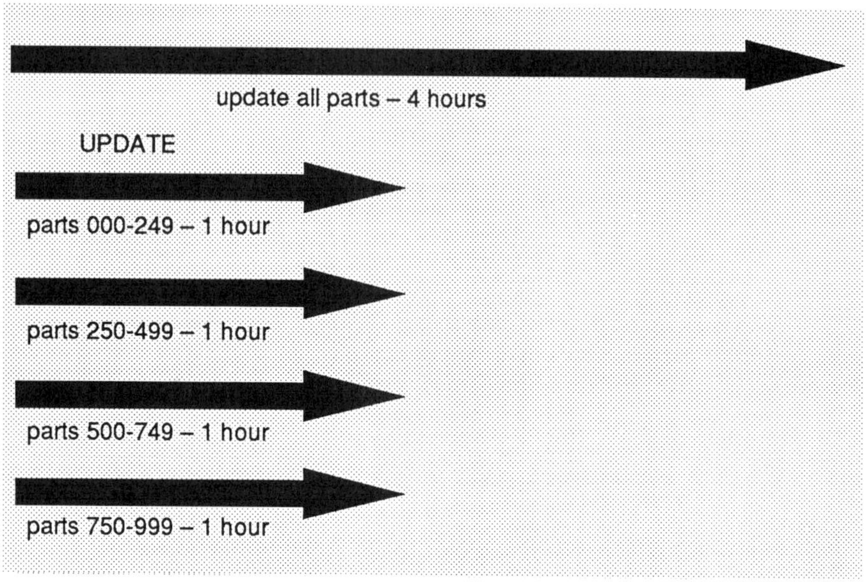

FIGURE 38. Breaking up a long run into a series of short runs.

- Update contention is minimized because ORACLE considers the data bases to be separate and distinct.
- The opportunity to physically spread processing over multiple processors is heightened because data can be processed independently.

Of course, when the designer breaks data into physically smaller and physically separate data bases, then the processing strategy naturally follows. For example, if a data base were broken by geographic location, the batch processing would not be broken along the lines of marketing divisions. In other words, the major divisions of data must apply throughout the organization.

PEAK-PERIOD PROCESSING

The batch window typically has its peak-period processing moments, just like the online window. And, as with the online window, the consequences of not anticipating peak-period requirements in the batch window can be severe.

When the batch window must be extended, either the online window does not come up as scheduled or the amount of work done in the batch window is shortchanged.

The peak periods for the batch window typically include month-end processing, year-end processing, business cycle peak periods, and so forth. It is worth the ORACLE application designer's time to anticipate these peak periods. There are several options the designer has:

- Split processing (if possible) across more than one processor.
- Reduce peak-period processing by altering the application workload. For example, a bank may produce statements for its customers once a month, but may do so in independent cycles so that on any given working day only a fraction of the customers have statements produced.

SMALL DATA BASES

In many other contexts, the usefulness of physically small data bases has been noted. In the management of the batch window, small data bases are likewise quite useful. If there is an overriding design requirement in ORACLE for the management of the batch window, it is that data bases be kept as physically small as possible.

Small data bases:

- Allow the largest amount of freedom in the structuring of the job-stream in the batch window.
- Affect (beneficially) not just application batch processing but utilities as well.
- Give the operator managing the batch window the most flexibility in ending or extending the batch window.
- Reduce the amount of work needed in reprocessing and/or backing out data in a recovery, in the event of a failure.
- Automatically reduce the set size that is processed by an ORACLE SQL statement.
- Provide opportunities for parallel processing on separate processors where applicable.
- Can be tailored to a specific user's needs rather than having to generically fit a large population of users.

In short, the advantages of physically small data bases far outweigh the disadvantages and are strongly advised for the management of the batch window.

SUMMARY

The batch environment for ORACLE is as important as the online environment. If batch processing extends into the online processing day, the performance implications are obvious.

Planning for the batch window begins with an estimation of how long the window needs to be open, both on the average and in the worst case. The requirements of the batch window are compared with the business requirements of the online day.

Some techniques for minimizing/streamlining processing in the batch window are:

- Minimizing the need for relational joins. Usually, relational joins require many more resources than simple sort and merges.
- Creating parallel runs. The elapsed time can be significantly shrunk when a long run can be broken into a series of shorter runs that can be run in parallel.

QUESTIONS: THE ORACLE BATCH ENVIRONMENT

1. The production environment has two major divisions: online processing and ______________ processing.
2. Long sequential processes are run during the ______________ window.
3. The batch window is ALWAYS/SOMETIMES during off-peak hours.
4. Online processing is hampered when the batch window extends into the online day. (T/F)
5. If the batch window is not long enough, either it must be extended or batch jobs that are scheduled to run must not be run. (T/F)
6. The length of the batch window varies SUBSTANTIALLY/ONLY SLIGHTLY.
7. The length of the batch window needs to be estimated as part of the design of the APPLICATION/ENTIRE BATCH ENVIRONMENT.

8. Estimates of batch processing may take into account buffer "hits" due to sequential processing. (T/F)
9. Batch I/Os are done in THE SAME/LESS THAN THE/MORE THAN THE time range in relation to online I/Os.
10. Data base design for batch is AS/LESS/MORE important vis á vis online systems.
11. Name some typical activities that run during the batch window.
12. Data base joins are no problem in the batch environment. (T/F)
13. For a large data base, a sort and merge procedure is OFTEN/SELDOM more efficient than a join.
14. Parallel sequential runs can be executed when the same data IS/IS NOT needed by two or more runs.
15. Parallel runs have the potential of being run on ________ processors.
16. Most DSS data bases are periodically fed by a batch process known as an ________ program.
17. Extracted data is sent to the dss environment for ________ processing and analysis.
18. There may be great economies of processing if there is much extract processing and if all the extracts against a given data base are combined into a ________ extract.
19. Extracting as much data as might be needed, not merely the amount specified by the analyst, often saves ________.
20. Saving extract files until the next major extract:
    a. can save unexpected processing
    b. wastes space
    c. is overly cautious
21. When batch job A updates a data base and batch job B reports from the data base, then job A MUST/MIGHT be run before B.
22. There is USUALLY/ALWAYS/SOMETIMES a mandatory sequencing of batch jobs.
23. When there is no mandatory sequence of execution of batch jobs, then the jobs can be ________.
24. Typical periods of peak batch processing come at ________, ________ end, etc.
25. The analyst must account for peak-period batch processing as well as peak-period online processing. (T/F)

CHAPTER 9

Archival Processing and ORACLE

Archival processing usually is not a production data processing environment in most companies. (Of course, in a few organizations, archival processing forms the backbone of the work of the company.) But even when archival processing does not form the basis of the mainstream application production processing, archival processing usually enhances and complements it. Separating work and data into the archival environment frees up resources for higher-priority production application processing.

CRITERIA FOR SUCCESS IN ARCHIVAL PROCESSING

The criteria for success of the archival environment are very different from those for other environments. High performance, high availability over long periods of time, rapid system development, and so forth, are normally not high-priority criteria in the archival environment, as they are in other environments. Only the management of large amounts of data is a criterion of success shared by the archival and typical application production environments.

In the archival environment, there are usually massive amounts of data—even larger volumes than those found in the largest production environment. The management of very large amounts of data is perhaps the single most important criterion of success in the archival environment.

The nature of archival processing is the storage of large amounts of data for future, unknown needs. Traditionally, analysis of archival data has been done heuristically. There are essentially two types of heuristic archival processing: processing to find a few records out of many or processing massive amounts of records. For example, the archival analyst may search a company's files and records to locate all sales made in New Mexico, where state tax has been calculated at 3.5 percent between the first of May 1962 and the sixth of July 1962. Only a few records will satisfy these criteria, and the search is like looking for the needle in a haystack.

The other type of archival analysis is the search for and manipulation of massive amounts of data. For example, the archival analyst might wish to determine the average length of time between purchases for those customers making multiple purchases between 1981 and 1985. The satisfaction of this analysis requires much movement and manipulation of data.

ARCHIVAL MEDIA

The medium on which archival data is stored has a profound influence on the analysis that can be done. Archival storage media fall into two categories: electronic reproducible and nonelectronic reproducible. An example of an electronic reproducible medium is magnetic tape or standard DASD.

An example of a nonelectronic reproducible medium is microfiche. Once data is put off onto microfiche, searches for single records can be done fairly efficiently if the key of the record desired is known. However, massive access and manipulation of data is expensive and awkward in microfiche. Data on nonelectronic reproducible media is inexpensive to store and is relatively secure from damage.

When data is placed on an electronic reproducible medium, massive manipulation of the data can be done (as well as searches for single records). The cost of storage on electronic reproducible medium is relatively high, and on occasion, whole volumes of data become damaged and are not easily replaced or restored.

Based upon the type of archival analysis that needs to be done, the appropriate medium must be selected. If massive manipulation of archival data is to be done, then an electronically reproducible medium should be selected.

Far and above all other issues, the management of a great many volumes of data is the overriding issue of archival processing. And not only are there massive amounts of archival data, but at the rate at which archival data grows, the volumes of data mount rapidly.

PRIMITIVE ARCHIVAL DATA

The most effective storage of archival data is at the primitive level (Refer to *Data Architecture: The Information Paradigm*, QED Information Sciences Inc., 1989, for an in-depth discussion of primitive data). Since archival data is stored for unknown usage, the most basic, most detailed data needs to be stored. The lower the level of detail stored, the greater the chance that future unknown processing needs will be satisfied. If a unit of data is not stored for future archival needs, then it is permanently lost (i.e., when any primitive unit of data is deleted from the production environment, if the unit is not archived, it is permanently lost).

Derived data can be stored in the archival environment as well. But most data stored there is primitive. Once detailed, primitive data is archived, the data forms the basis for reconciliation of dss processing and other archival analysis at a later time.

PHYSICAL DEFINITION

Archival data should be stored with as "universal" a physical definition as possible. In other words, the physical layout (i.e., the definition) of archival data should be stored in a manner that will facilitate future retrieval. A simple character definition of a field may waste some space, but will simplify future analysts' jobs when they try to use the data. The physical format of the archived data should be in the most popular and widely used form possible.

In addition to the content of data being archived, the format (i.e., the semantics and the structure) of data should be archived as well. The format should contain the field name, the data characteristics, and any pertinent information about the field that will help future archival analysts understand the meaning and content of the data that has been stored. Any tables or coding structures should likewise be referenced and stored.

In general, data relationships in archival files are kept to a minimum if they are kept at all.

SUBJECT ORIENTATION

The orientation of archival data is toward the major subjects of the organization, as are the standard operational data bases derived from the business of the enterprise. Over time, detailed, process-oriented aspects of the major subjects of the enterprise are sure to change, but the major subjects themselves are slow to change. The orientation of the archival data bases to the major subjects of the organization (which is the same orientation as the operational data bases) provides a straightforward basis for the flow of data from the operational to the archival environment.

At first glance, the applicability of ORACLE to archival data is severely limited. The volume of data, the infrequency of access, and the inability to predict the usage of the data all present special problems to the ORACLE archival analyst. For example, sheer volume normally precludes the indexing of *any* of the data, a severe limitation to the usefulness of the ORACLE software. Another problem is that the masses of data stored before ORACLE became widely available may not be able to be conveniently translated into a format known to ORACLE. Even if a conversion from an existing format to an ORACLE format can be done, the overhead entailed is potentially very large. As a consequence, ORACLE is not generally applicable to the standard archival environment.

THE LIVING SAMPLE ENVIRONMENT

There is one archival environment, however, to which ORACLE is peculiarly applicable. It is called the "living sample" environment, and ORACLE is truly an ideal tool for it.

The living sample environment is best described in terms of some examples. Suppose an archival analyst analyzes ten years of historical data. He or she determines that the average sale over the 10-year period was $105.36, that the busiest time of the year was December 16, and that 87 percent of sales were conducted with credit cards. To arrive at those conclusions, the archival analyst goes through 750,000 individual transactions that occurred from 1976 to 1986.

Now suppose another analyst is operating from a living sample archival data base. A living sample data base is made up of representative samples of data and is periodically refreshed (thus the term "living sample"). There are 10,000 representative transactions in the living sample data base, and operating against it, the archival analyst determines that the average sale is $104.96, that the busiest time of the year is December 17, and that 85.6 percent of business is conducted through credit cards.

There is no doubt that the first archival analyst has a more accurate answer than the second one. But there is likewise no doubt that the cost of processing actual archival data is *very* expensive, and the worth of total accuracy is questionable. The living sample analyst has arrived at very close to the same conclusion as the archival analyst, but the living sample analyst has processed one-seventy fifth the records. Unless there is a need for an unusually high degree of accuracy, the second analyst using living sample data has arrived at satisfactory conclusions much more efficiently than the analyst using classical archival data. The accuracy of the estimate can be made using standard statistical sampling techniques.

ORACLE is an ideal tool for living sample analysis. There is not so much data in the living sample environment that it cannot be managed by ORACLE. Indexes can be created as data is periodically refreshed. The living sample dss analyst in ORACLE has the full gamut of ORACLE options with which to analyze data.

Furthermore, many of the constraints of the production environment, such as using "designed" transactions, are not necessary in the living sample environment.

Some Design Considerations—Time Stamping Data

Practically all of the data in the living sample environment will be "time stamped." A time stamp is merely an appendage of the key indicating the value or status of a key as of some moment in time. For example, an account may be archived periodically. In September 1986, Account 3650 contained $1584.00. The domicile of the account is the Market Street branch, and the date the account was opened was May 1979. The key of the record is account/year/month. On the first of October a "snapshot" of the September data is taken and is archived.

There are two ways archived data is time stamped: with a discrete time value and with a continuous time value. A discrete time value represents a single point in time, as previously discussed for an account. A continuous time value has a beginning and an end and represents data as having the values contained for the entire length of time measured by the continuous dates. For example, the bank pays 5.5 percent interest on passbook accounts from January 1985 to July 1987. A continuous time-stamp record would look like: key—account type, beginning date, ending date; nonkey—interest rate, other terms.

Continuous time stamping is most appropriate to small numbers of data elements that change infrequently. Every time a variable changes values, a new continuous record must be created.

Continuous data normally maintains a simple continuity—where the ending date of the earlier record is one unit of time less than the beginning date of the later continuous record. But simple continuity is not the only choice. On occasion discontinuous or overlapping records may need to be kept.

Another consideration is the beginning date of the first continuous time-span record and the ending date of the last continuous time-span record. These dates may have an actual value or may be open ended. For example, if the ending date for the last continuous time-span record equals infinity, then the time-span information is valid indefinitely, until further update can occur. But if the ending date has a value, then the set of continuous records has a finite ending.

Discrete snapshot data is applicable to large amounts of data that rapidly change (as opposed to continuous time-span data). A major concern of discrete time-variant data is the frequency of snapshots. Snapshots taken too frequently will be voluminous and may actually mask long-term trends. Snapshots taken not frequently enough will lose important fluctuations of data.

An issue applicable to both discrete and continuously measured data is that of the unit of measurement. For example, a measurement of a checking account balance by year does not make sense; nor does the measurement of the Dow Jones Industrial Average by the minute. The unit of time used to measure time-variant data must be appropriate to it.

One of the disciplines of the creation of the living sample environment is in the preservation of its complete data needs. Very often, archival data is made up of the "refuse" of the operational environment. Only those data elements that are being purged from the operational environment are sent to the archival environment.

While newly purged data may well belong in the archival environment, other data that may not be purged ought to be there as well in order to present a clear picture for archival processing. Establishing and using the living sample environment brings to light the complete set of needs of the archival analyst. Another advantage of ORACLE in the living sample environment is its orientation towards set processing. The time stamping that occurs arranges data conveniently into sets.

To see how ORACLE tables might be processed as time-variant tables, consider the following examples.

Two tables are defined to ORACLE containing archival data. One, the account table, contains account identification, the balance of the account as of the fifteenth of the month, and the type of loan. Figure 39 shows the layout of the data for the account table.

The table in Figure 39 is recognized as discrete time-variant data. The loan table contains continuous time-variant data. The loan table contains a key of loan type and the beginning date and ending date of the loan, as well as the effective rate during the time span. The loan rows are arranged so that they continuously define all the days of the year. In other words, the beginning date of row $n+1$ is one day less than the ending date of row n. Figure 40 shows the table layout for the loan table.

There are several other variables that are needed. Cumulative rate is simply the variable used to store values that will be calculated. The variable 'CALCDATE' is used to control the iterations of the algorithm. Figure 41 shows the definitions of the variables.

Some sample occurrences of the account and the rate table are shown by Figure 42.

The account table and the loan table are relationally defined, but they cannot be joined in the normal sense. Even though the date fields enjoy a logical intersection of data, the actual physical join is more difficult to implement.

Consider a simple logical join. Suppose the interest paid for an account for a year is to be calculated. The balance in one table is to be multiplied by the applicable rate in the other table. The algorithm shown in Figure 43 merges the two tables based on the intersection of dates.

ACCT	char (10)
DATE	
MONTH	number (2,0)
DAY	number (2,0)
TYPE	char (1)
BALANCE	number (9,2)

FIGURE 39. Data layout for the acct/balance table.

LOAN TYPE	CHAR (1)
BEG DATE	
YEAR	number (2,0)
MONTH	number (2,0)
DAY	number (2,0)
END DATE	
YEAR	number (2,0)
MONTH	number (2,0)
DAY	number (2,0)
RATE	number (5,4)

FIGURE 40. A table layout for discrete time-variant data.

Twelve calculations are made for an account for a year. The rate that is applicable as of the fifteenth of the month is multiplied by the balance and is divided by 12 (there are twelve accumulations made per year). The value accumulated in CUMRATE roughly approximates the interest paid by an account for a year.

But a finer calculation may be required. The simple calculation made for each month assumes that the interest rate is constant from

CALC DATE	
YEAR	number (2,0)
MONTH	number (2,0)
DAY	number (2,0)
CUM RATE	number (11,9)

FIGURE 41. Definitions of variables for discrete time-variant data.

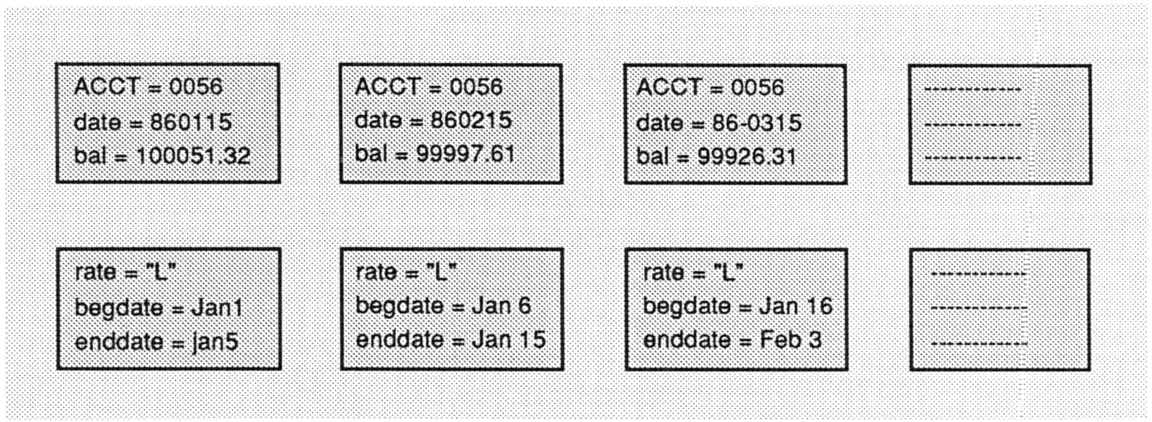

FIGURE 42. Sample occurrences of the account and rate tables with discrete time-variant data.

```
CUMRATE = 0
CALCMONTH = 1
CALCDAY = 15
DO WHILE CALCMONTH < 13
    SELECT ACCTBALANCE ACCTTYPE
    FROM ACCTTABLE
    WHERE ACCT = 'xxx...' AND ACCTDATE = CALCDATE
    SELECT LOANRATE
    FROM RATETABLE
    WHERE LOANTYPE = ACCTTYPE 'ND
        LOANBEGDATE =< CALCDATE AND
        LOANENDDATE >= CALCDATE
    CUMRATE = CUMRATE+
        ((LOANRATE x ACCTBALANCE)/12)
    CALCMONTH = CALCMONTH +1
END
```

FIGURE 43. Algorithm for merging two tables based on intersection of dates.

the fifteenth of the month being calculated to the fifteenth of the next month. But such is not the case. The rate is variable and may change many times throughout the month. A finer, more precise calculation, done on a day-by-day basis, is shown by Figure 44.

In Figure 44, each day's interest is calculated. If rates change, a new SQL call is made to retrieve the new daily rate.

The example shows how two time-variant files can be "joined" logically even though a physical join is not possible. The balance file is time stamped with discrete data, and the rate file is time stamped with continuous data. And they are logically merged based on matching key values and logically intersecting data values.

But logical joins are not the only challenge facing the archival analyst.

```
CUMRATE = 0
CALCMONTH = 1
CALCDAY = 15
DO WHILE CALCMONTH < 13
DO WHILE CALCMONTH < 13
    SELECT ACCTBALANCE ACCTTYPE
    FROM ACCTTABLE
    WHERE ACCT = 'xxx...' AND ACCTDATE = CALCDATE
    SELECT LOANRATE
    FROM RATETABLE
    WHERE LOANTYPE = ACCTTYPE AND
        LOANBEGDATE =< CALCDATE AND
        LOANENDDATE >= CALCDATE
    DAYPROG = 'N'
    DO WHILE DAYPROG = 'N'
        CUMRATE = CUMRATE+
          ((ACCTBALANCE x LOANRATE)/365)
        CALCDAY = CALCDAY+1
        IF CALCDAY = 32 AND IF CALCMONTH = 1 THEN DO
            CALCMONTH = 2
            CALCDAY = 1
            END
        IF CALCDAY = 29 THEN IF CALCMONTH = 2 THEN DO
            CALCMONTH = 3
            CALCDAY = 1
            END
```

FIGURE 44. A precise calculation, done on a day-by-day basis, of an account's interest.

```
IF CALCDAY = 31 THEN IF CALCMONTH = 3 THEN DO
      CALCMONTH = 4
      CALCDAY = 1
      END
      --------------------------------------------------------------
      --------------------------------------------------------------
      --------------------------------------------------------------
IF CALCDAY > LOANENDDATE THEN DO
      SELECT LOANRATE
      FROM RATETABLE
      WHERE LOANTYPE = ACCTTYPE AND
            LOANBEGDATE =< CALCDATE
            AND LOANENDDATE >= CALCDATE
      END
IF CALCDATE = 15 THEN DAYCALC = 'Y'
END
```

FIGURE 44. Continued

EFFICIENT ACCESS OF ARCHIVAL DATA

Some problems are endemic to the archival environment. Although the problems will be illustrated within the context of ORACLE processing, it is noted that *any* data management software could experience the same problems.

One problem facing the archival analyst is the arrangement of data so that efficient access can be made. This is the same problem facing the analyst in other circumstances, except that in the case of archival data the massive amounts of data and the way the data is collected and accessed presents some peculiar problems.

As an example, suppose that each month on the fifteenth, account balance information is stripped from production files. The bulk of the data will be loaded into an archival file. If the data is unindexed in the archival file (which is extremely likely because there is normally so much data that no indexes can be built), it will be loaded in a sequential fashion. Assuming that the data is loaded sequentially (i.e., in the same sequence as collected), Figure 45 shows how a physical page might look after being loaded from the January strip.

There is nothing inherently wrong with the approach of simply loading data to an archival file as stripped and time stamped. But consider the result of this process as it places data over several pages, as shown by Figure 46.

Consider the work done by the system to analyze the balance of a given account over several months or years. The system must go to a new page for every month's activity. Twelve I/Os will be needed to access 12 months' data for an account even if ORACLE knows which pages the data resides in.

If it appears that single-account analysis will be a normal archival activity (i.e., an analytical activity that occurs on a fairly frequent basis), then a different organization of data is required.

The data needs to be physically colocated based on account/data. But merely colocating the data (assuming that the data *can* be colocated!) may not be adequate. Unless *much* free space is left in the page when the first entry is inserted, the colocation of data can lead to horrendous data management problems as later inserts are made.

In order to colocate, the data can be loaded in the following manner. On the January load (assuming the archival data bases are created in January), the data for the month of January is entered. At the same time, dummy entries are inserted for February, March, and so forth. The dummy entries contain key values and default values (such as 0) for nonkey data. Figure 47 shows a few pages after the January load.

In February (and in subsequent months) data is replaced, not

ACCT	001	002	003	004	----------
DATE	Jan15	Jan15	Jan15	Jan15	----------
Balance	nnnn	nnnn	nnnn	nnnn	----------

FIGURE 45. Data in a page after a sequential, unclustered loading.

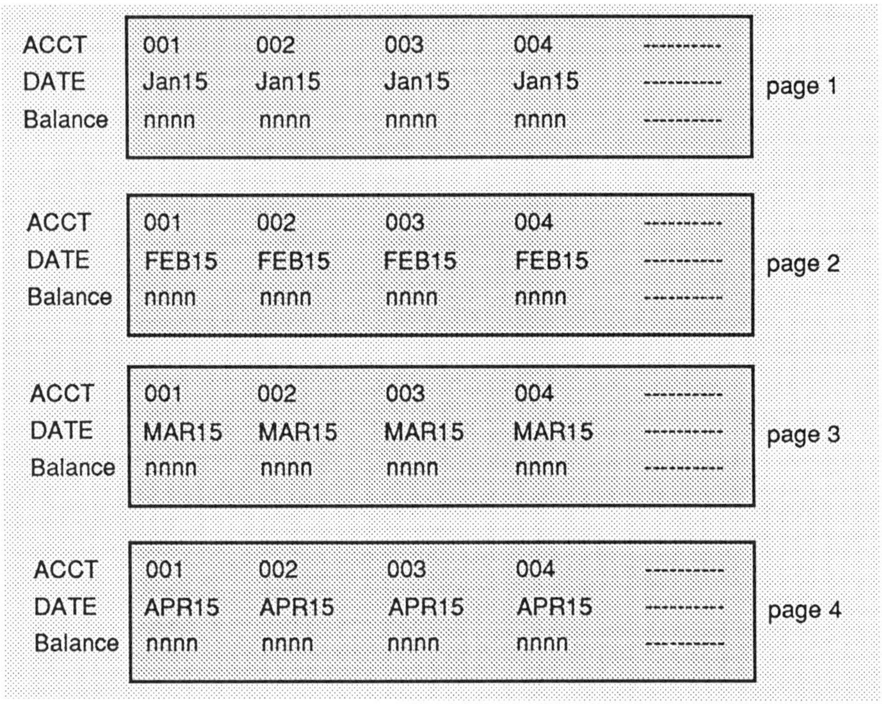

FIGURE 46. Data after having been loaded once a month.

inserted. With the resulting organization of data, a single account's activity can be accessed in one I/O, not twelve.

Storage and management of data that occurs or is measured at predictable intervals are relatively simple. Data that occurs or is measured randomly presents entirely different problems to the archival analyst and designer.

For example, suppose an archival analyst wishes to store information about the checks written by banking customers. Some customers write many more checks than other customers. And the number of checks written one month may vary significantly from another month for a single customer.

One approach is simply to store, by month, all the checks written by all customers. All the checks written are gathered into a monthly file. The gathering of the information is easy and natural, but the utilization of the files can present fearsome problems. To retrieve

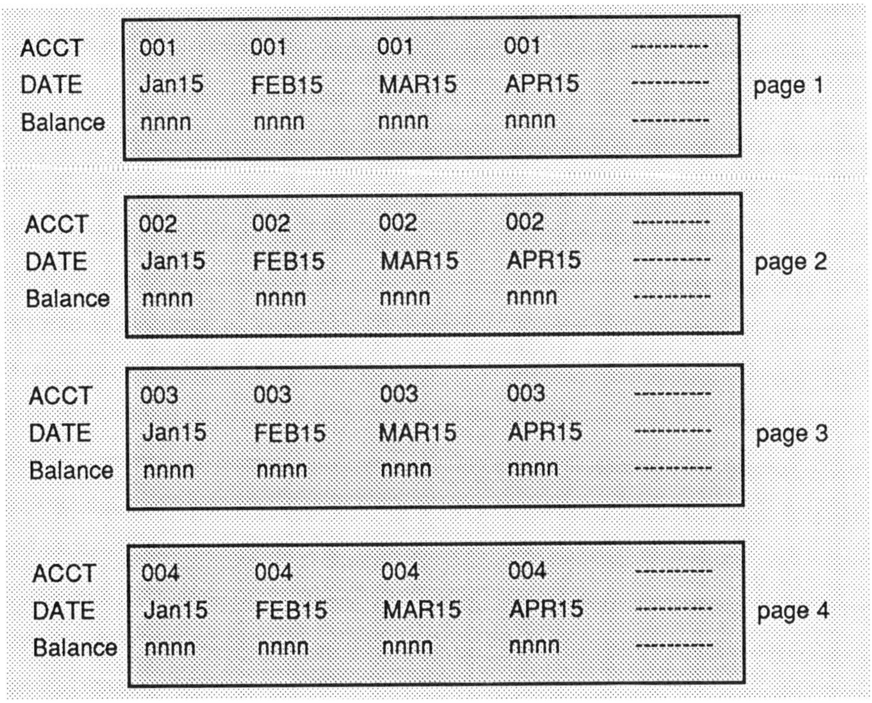

FIGURE 47. Data loaded monthly, with dummy entries inserted at the first of the year.

information, the first qualifications must be on date (or at least month). For some types of processing, this division of data may not be much of a problem. But consider the work the analyst must do in tracking the customer's running balance from one month to the next.

A second option is to reserve as much space as is normally needed for a customer for a year. Each month the checking activities are loaded into the space reserved for them, by individual customer account. But there are some problems with this approach. Suppose 35 "slots" are allocated each month for each customer's checking activity. One month a customer has used only 15 slots. What happens to the unused slots? Another month a customer uses (or needs) 60 slots. Where do the extra slots come from?

These questions can certainly be answered, but the complexity and management challenges can be severe.

INTEGRITY AND ACCURACY OF ARCHIVAL DATA

Another typical problem facing the designer is that of maintaining integrity and accuracy of data. For example, consider the problems of the programmer in the maintenance of continuous time-span data. Updates or creations of data can cause very complex problems when one or more rows of data participate in a continuous definition of a time span. For example, Figure 48 shows some continuous time-span rows.

In the data shown in Figure 48, rate type = "L," loan limit = 1000, and the rate varies from day to day. Each of the rows begins one unit beyond where the previous row ends. In other words, the first row's logical end is on January 6. The next beginning date must be January 7, otherwise there would be a discontinuity of the data. Note, too, that there is no overlap of data defined by two or more rows. In other words, for any given point in time defined by the continuous time span, there is one and only one set of values that are applicable.

Now suppose the following transaction is entered: Change the limit value of loans to 1500 for the dates of January 4 to January 20. In this case transaction variables are TX.BEG = January 4, TX.BEG = January 20, and TX.LIMIT = 1500. TX.RATE = 0 (or null values), indicating that rate is not affected by the transaction.

The data after the update has been applied to the continuous time span shown in Figure 48 is shown in Figure 49.

Several new rows have been created, and some existing rows have been updated. The continuity of the data remains the same.

The data was updated by means of the following algorithm: Suppose the transaction has a beginning and ending date of TX.BEG and

RATE TYPE	L	L	L	L	--------
DATES	0101-0106	0107-0214	0215-0228	0228-0301	--------
RATE	.053	.058	.061	.063	--------
LIMIT	1000	1000	1000	1000	--------

FIGURE 48. Continuous time-span rows.

L	L	L	L	L	--------
0101-0103	0104-0106	0107-0120	0121=0214	0215-0228	--------
.053	.053	.058	.058	.061	--------
1000	1500	1500	1000	1000	--------

FIGURE 49. Continuous time-span data after update has been applied.

TX.END. If a nonkey field is to be updated—in this case LIMIT and RATE—the field to be transacted has a value greater than zero. If a nonkey field is not to be updated it has a null value.

Suppose the ORACLE table has (for the data portion of the key) the field DB.BEG. For the purposes of the algorithm to be discussed, assume that the RATE.TYPE of the key has been satisfied (in other words, assume that only the continuous dates must be matched between the transaction and the data base).

The continuous time-span data base is indexed, with a data layout shown by Figure 50.

Note that the key of the data base is the beginning date, not the beginning and ending date. Ending date is not needed for uniqueness.

The alogrithm needed to service the continuous time-span data structure is shown in Figure 51.

FOREIGN KEYS IN THE ARCHIVAL ENVIRONMENT

Foreign key relationships are complicated by the volume of data over which the keys interrelate data, and the appendage of data onto the key structure of otherwise normal, straightforward relationships. The volume of data and the infrequency of access under normal circumstances:

BEGDATE		
YEAR	number (2,0)	key
MONTH	number (2,0)	key
DATE	number (2,0)	key
ENDDATE		
YEAR	number (2,0)	
MONTH	number (2,0)	
DATE	number (2,0)	
RATE	number (5,0)	
LIMIT	number (11,2)	

FIGURE 50. Data layout of continuous time-span data.

```
START:  SELECT DB.BEG DB.END DB.BALANCE DB.LIMIT
        FROM RATE.TABLE
        WHERE DB.BEG <=: TX.BEG AND DB.END >=: TX.BEG

    IF TX.BEG < DB.BEG AND IF TX.END < DB.END THEN DO
        NEWRATE = TX.RATE
        NEW LIMIT = TX.LIMIT
        INSERT INTO RATE.TABLE
        VALUES (TX.BEG, DB.BEG -1, NEWRATE, NEWLIMIT)
        ROWBEG = DB.BEG
        NEWRATE = DB.RATE
        IF TX.RATE > 0 THEN NEWRATE = TX.RATE
        NEW LIMIT = DB.LIMIT
        IF TX.LIMIT > 0 THEN NEW LIMIT = DB.LIMIT
        UPDATE RATETABLE
        SET DB.END =: TX.END
           DB.RATE=: NEWRATE
           DB.LIMIT =: NEWLIMIT
           WHERE DB.BEG =: ROWBEG
            INSERT INTO RATE.TABLE
        VALUES (TX.END + 1, DB.END, DB.RATE, DB.LIMIT)
        END
    IF TX.BEG < DB.BEG AND IF TX.END = DB.END THEN DO
        NEWRATE = TX.RATE
        NEWLIMIT = TX.LIMIT
        INSERT INTO RATE.TABLE
        VALUES (TX.BEG, DB.BEG-1, NEW.RATE, NEW.LIMIT)
        ROWBEG = DB.BEG
        NEW RATE = DB.RATE
        IF TX.RATE > 0 THEN NEWRATE = TX.RATE
        NEWLIMIT = DB.LIMIT
        IF TX.LIMIT > 0 THEN NEW RATE = TX. RATE
        UPDATE RATE.TABLE
        SET DB.END =: TX.END
           DB.RATE =: NEWRATE
           DB.LIMIT =: NEWLIMIT
           WHERE DB.BEG =: ROWBEG
        END
```

FIGURE 51. Algorithm needed to service continuous time-span data structure.

```
IF TX.BEG = DB.BEG AND IF TX.END > DB.END THEN DO;
   NEWRATE = DB.RATE
   NEWLIMIT = DB.LIMIT
   IF TX.RATE >0 THEN NEWRATE = TX.RATE
   IF TX.LIMIT >0 THEN NEWLIMIT = TX.LIMIT
   UPDATE RATE.TABLE
   SET DB.RATE =: NEWRATE
   DB.LIMIT =: NEWLIMIT
   WHERE DB.BEG =: TX.BEG
   TX.BEG = DB.END +1
   GO TO START
   END
IF TX.BEG > DB.BEG THEN IF TX.END < DB.END THEN DO
   ROWBEG = DB.BEG
   UPDATE RATE.TABLE
   SET DB.END =: TX.BEG -1
   WHERE DB.BEG =: ROWBEG
   NEWRATE = DB.RATE
   NEWLIMIT = DB.LIMIT
   IF TX.RATE >0 THEN NEWRATE = TX.RATE
   IF TX.LIMIT >0 THEN NEWLIMIT = TX.LIMIT
   INSERT INTO RATE.TABLE
   VALUES (TX.BEG, TX.END, NEWRATE, NEWLIMIT)
   INSERT INTO RATE.TABLE
   VALUES (TX.END + 1, DB.END, DB.RATE, DB.LIMIT)
   END
IF TX.BEG >DB.BEG THEN IF TX.END = DB.END THEN DO
   ROWBEG = DB.BEG
   UPDATE RATE.TABLE
   SET DB.END =: TX.BEG -1
   WHERE DB.END =: ROWBEG
   NEWRATE = DB.RATE
   NEWLIMIT = DB.LIMIT
   IF TX.RATE >0 THEN NEWRATE = TX.RATE
   IF TX.LIMIT >0 THEN NEWLIMIT = TX.LIMIT
   INSERT INOT RATE.TABLE
    VALUES (TX.BEG, TX.END, NEWRATE, NEWLIMIT)
   END
```

Figure 51. Continued

```
IF TX.BEG < DB.BEG AND IF TX.END > DB.END THEN DO
   NEWRATE = TX.RATE
   NEWLIMIT = TX.LIMIT
   INSERT INTO RATE.TABLE
   VALUES (TX.BEG, DB.BEG - 1, NEWRATE, NEW.LIMIT)
   ROWBEG = DB.BEG
   NEWRATE = DB.RATE
   NEWLIMIT = DB.LIMIT
   IF TX.RATE >0 THEN NEWRATE = TX.RATE
   IF TX.LIMIT >0 THEN NEWLIMIT = TX.LIMIT
   UPDATE RATE.TABLE
   SET DB.RATE =: NEWRATE
      DB.LIMIT =:NEWLIMIT
      WHERE DB.BEG =: ROWBEG
   TX.BEG = DB.END +1
   GO TO START
   END
IF TX.BEG = DB.BEG AND IF TX.END<DB.END
   NEWRATE = DB.RATE
   NEWLIMIT = DB.LIMIT
   IF TX.RATE >0 THEN NEWRATE = TX.RATE
   IF TX.LIMIT > 0 THEN NEWLIMIT = TX.LIMIT
   UPDATE RATE.TABLE
   SET DB.END =: TX.END
      DB. LIMIT =: NEWLIMIT
      DB.RATE =: NEWRATE
      WHERE DB.BEG =: TX.BEG
   INSERT INTO RATE.TABLE
   VALUES (TX.END + 1, DB.END, DB.RATE, DB.LIMIT)
   END
IF TX.BEG = DB.BEG AND IF TX.END = DB.END THEN DO
   NEWRATE = DB.RATE
   NEWLIMIT = DB.LIMIT
   IF TX.RATE >0 THEN NEWRATE = TX.RATE
   IF TX.LIMIT >0 THEN NEWLIMIT = TX.LIMIT
   UPDATE RATE.TABLE
   SET DB.RATE =:NEWRATE
      DB.LIMIT =: NEWLIMIT
      WHERE DB.BEG =: TX.BEG
   END
```

Figure 51. Continued

```
IF TX.BEG > DB.BEG THEN IF TX.END >DB.END THEN DO
   ROWBEG = DB.BEG
   UPDATE RATE.TABLE
   SET DB.END =: TX.BEG -1
   WHERE DB.END =: ROWBEG
   NEWRATE = DB.RATE
   NEWLIMIT= DB.LIMIT
   IF TX.RATE >0 THEN NEWRATE = TX.RATE
   IF TX.LIMIT >0 THEN NEWLIMIT = TX.LIMIT
   INSERT INTO RATE.TABLE
   VALUES (TX.BEG, DB.END, NEWRATE, NEWLIMIT)
   TX.BEG = DB.END + 1
   GO TO START
   END
```

Figure 51. Continued

- Preclude the usage of an index.
- Preclude the usage of a cross-reference table.

The remaining choice for relating tables together—dynamically creating the relationship by scanning volumes of data—is likewise unpopular in the face of very large volumes of data. Furthermore, the appendage of data with time stamps—either discrete or continuous—on each key creates logical intersections of data that cannot be joined in the normal manner.

Clearly, special design techniques are required to manage foreign keys in the face of the ORACLE archival environment. Some design techniques that can be used separately or in tandem are:

- Sectioning ORACLE data into smaller data bases so that standard foreign key relationships can be implemented.
- Creating "selective" cross-reference tables, joining selected parts or subsets of tables, not all rows. The selectivity criteria may be on high-dollar items, selected "special" or trouble accounts, etc.
- Creating time-dependent cross-reference tables (as opposed to general-purpose cross references). For example, for the year 1986 one cross reference can be created. Another cross reference can be created for 1987, and so forth.
- Creating selective intersection copies of data that require no further joins. Instead of creating cross references, data is duplicated and actual intersection tables are created. It must be kept in mind that when data is duplicated (especially archived data), the data must conform to the architectural rules for the management of atomic data.

SUMMARY

ORACLE is applicable to the archival environment when "living sample" processing of archival data is done. In other cases, the volume of data prevents the usage of many ORACLE features, such as indexing.

Archival data is normally time stamped. Time-variant data that is time stamped requires special handling. For example, the standard joins of ORACLE cannot be done with time-stamped data in the normal manner. Special algorithms are required to logically actuate the join.

Time-stamped data is either continuous or discrete. The volatility of the data, the number of data elements, the usage of the data, etc., all contribute to the decision of how to manage time-variant data.

QUESTIONS: ARCHIVAL PROCESSING AND ORACLE

1. Production processing usually DOES/DOES NOT involve archival data and processing.
2. A good criterion to determine what is and is not archival is ______________.
3. The criteria for success in the operational environment—high performance and high availability—ARE/ARE NOT the same criteria for success in the archival environment.
4. There usually is MORE/LESS data in the archival environment than in the operational environment.
5. The nature of processing against archival data can be described as ______________.
6. The medium on which archival data is stored has a ______________ effect on the processing that can occur.
7. Name some typical media on which archival data is stored.
8. The media on which archival data is stored can be classified into two camps: ______________ and ______________ .
9. Anelectronic reproducible medium is MORE/LESS expensive than electronic nonreproducible media.
10. Searching an electronic nonreproducible medium is MORE/LESS expensive than searching an electronic reproducible medium.
11. It is common practice to store mostly PRIMITIVE/DERIVED data at the archival level.
12. Derived data CAN/CANNOT be stored at the archival level.
13. Why is primitive data the best choice for archival storage?
14. Not only the content but the ______________ of data should be stored at the archival level.
15. ______________ should be stored as well.
16. Archival data, like operational data, is organized along the lines of the major ______________.
17. Because of the volume of data in the archival environment, it is very difficult to ______________ the data.
18. Because indexes are so limited, the possibilities for using ORACLE are limited.(T/F)
19. The living sample environment is a ______________ of the archival environment.

20. For certain types of processing, such as statistical analysis, living sample data bases are much more efficient than archival data bases. (T/F)

21. For other types of processing, such as ______________, living sample data bases are not adequate.

22. How appropriate is ORACLE to the living sample environment?

23. Practically all archival data and living sample data is ______________.

24. Time stamping usually means keys have a ______________ appended.

25. There are, in general, two methods of organizing time-stamped data: ______________ and ______________.

26. Organizing data according to existence dependency criteria produces a normalized data base design.

CHAPTER 10

Extract Processing in ORACLE

Extract processing is an integral part of the ORACLE environment. It is necessary to unlock the flexibility that can be achieved in ORACLE. There is nothing terribly difficult about extract processing from the standpoint of the programmer. The logic it requires is, for the most part, simple.

But extract processing soon becomes an issue given the volume of data that must pass through the extract programs. In short order, the amount of time required for extract processing begins to exceed the amount of time available. And the total amount of data that is being extracted soon overflows the available DASD. If not carefully thought out and carefully constructed, extract processing soon becomes a large issue in the running of an ORACLE environment.

Extract processing in ORACLE is done by application programs.

EXTRACT LOGIC

The logic required for extract processing is simple. The extract program is fed some parameters, which shape the logic that will be used to determine what data will be selected. Usually, the selection of data is from a production or operational data base or data bases.

Next the extract program accesses the original production data base(s) that serves as the source of data. The scan through the original data base may be sequential from one row to the next, or it may be by an index where the program logic is used to select values based on the contents of the index.

After data is selected by the extract program, it is transported to the output file. The output file may be in the same order as the original data, or it may be summarized, merged, or otherwise altered.

After the extract program has executed and the extracted output file is created, the analyst uses the extracted data as a basis for reports, for decision support analysis, for the creation of trend analysis files, or for other purposes.

The immediate challenge posed by extract processing is that it can consume a large amount of machine resources, principally in the usage of I/O. In addition, much DASD may be used for extracted files.

ARCHITECTING THE EXTRACT PROCESS

The first requirement in managing the extract process is not to do extracts in a random, disorganized manner. The extract of data from one environment to another represents a fundamental transformation of data with many implications in the usage, credibility, and efficiency of processing. (For an in-depth discussion of these issues refer to chapter 13, *Information Engineering for the Practitioner: From Theory Into Practice*, Yourdon Press, 1988.) The designer is well advised to carefully consider all the implications of extracts. In short, extract processing should not be an after-the-fact consideration in the design of the production and decision support ORACLE environments.

USING THE EXTRACTED DATA

In some cases, the ultimate use and disposition of the extracted data is well known. When the requirements are well established, the designer can design the content and occurrences of the extracted environment with precision. The goal in this case should be no wasted data, as each occurrence of extracted data requires storage and handling.

But in other instances, the usage and disposition of the extracted data is not known. In this case, the designer can only guess as to what data will be required. Even where there are unknown requirements for extracted data, it is worth the designer's while to try to anticipate requirements.

In the case of unknown requirements, if there is a lot of data to be managed, the designer will want to sort it into two categories: data that probably will be needed and data that probably will not be needed. The data that will be needed will be extracted and managed in the normal manner, but the data that probably will not be needed should be stored on a bulk archival medium. If the designer has guessed incorrectly, at a later point in time at least the data that has not been extracted will still be available. The problem is that restoring data from a bulk archival medium is awkward, slow, and expensive.

Of course, the designer can adopt the stance that all data needs to be extracted, regardless of the probability of access. Then he or she must pay the costs for unneeded storage and unneeded extract processing of data.

The designer should carefully consider the tradeoff between storing too little data and having to restore data from an awkward medium, and storing too much data and constantly paying the overhead for data that is never used.

GRANULARITY OF DATA

One of the most important issues the designer faces is the granularity of data as it is extracted. Data in the original (i.e., the unextracted state) is as granular as data is ever going to be. The designer may want to preserve the same level of granularity found in the unextracted state, or may want to summarize or otherwise consolidate the data. By consolidating the data upon extract, less I/O will be used for the loading of the extracted file and less DASD will be needed.

As an example of the considerations of the granularity of extracted data, consider a designer in a manufacturing environment who wants to extract data from the daily usage record for a parts file. Each withdrawal or replenishment of a part is recorded throughout the day in a production data base. One option for extract processing is simply to select each entry of data—each withdrawal and each replenishment—for the extract file. The extracted file can then be used to answer a host of questions, among them:

- What was the largest withdrawal during the day?
- What part had the most activities against it?
- At what time did the most withdrawals occur?

While these questions may be of interest, they require that data be stored in the extract file at the lowest level of granularity. Each withdrawal and replenishment must be captured and transported to the extract file. The number of records to be loaded and the amount of DASD required may be significant.

The designer could reduce the level of granularity in the extract file by storing cumulative withdrawal and replenishment activity by part. All daily withdrawals would be added with all daily replenishments for each part. Then the net activity for the day would be stored in the extract file. There would be no savings in the access of the original data, but much I/O would be saved in the writing out of the extract file. In addition, the output file would require much less DASD.

Of course, the analyst could not look at detailed transactions in the extract file, but he or she could still do much decision support analysis, such as looking at trends of parts usage.

The Right Level of Detail

There is no right or wrong answer as to what level of detail is appropriate for the extracted file. In general the designer should choose the highest level of detail (i.e., the most summarized level) that suffices for the queries that will be made against the data. The tradeoff is between the type of query that can be made and the cost of extracting and storing detailed data.

The granularity of extracted data and the processing that will be done against it, then, are the very first two issues that must be addressed by the designer.

Less Extracted Detail

Not only is the granularity of data an issue in the extraction of data; so is the level of detail that is extracted. While there may be cases where entire original records are shipped to an extracted environment, the designer should always assume that not all data elements are candidates for extraction.

For example, suppose a bank has a production data base where account activities are kept. A typical record in this data base contains the following data elements:

- Account identification
- Date, time of activity
- Amount of activity
- Location of activity
- Personal identification

- Teller window balance at time of activity
- Electronic identification
- Check number
- Any "posting" requested
- Any payroll activity

All of these data elements are required for operational processing and rightfully reside in the production data base. But it is unlikely that most of them belong in the extracted file. It is hard to imagine any sort of analytic processing of the extracted file that would require (or even find useful!) data elements such as check number or personal identification. The list of data elements in the original data base may thus be divided into two categories: those data elements needed for extracted processing and those not needed:

- Account identification [needed]
- Date, time of activity [needed]
- Amount of activity [needed]
- Location of activity [needed]
- Personal identification [not needed]
- Teller window balance at time of activity [not needed]
- Electronic identification [not needed]
- Check number [not needed]
- Any "posting" requested [not needed]
- Any payroll activity [not needed]

The amount of data shipped to the extract file then is only a subset of the original data, insofar as the type of data elements that are shipped is concerned. Of course, this weeding out does not make the scanning of the original data any more efficient, but it does make the loading of data (and its subsequent access!) more efficient, in that less data needs to be loaded. Loading less data implies that the data can be loaded more compactly. The tighter data can be loaded, the fewer resources are required in the loading and access of the data and the more quickly the load can be accomplished.

The granularity of the occurrences of data and the details that are shipped to the extract file, then, are two issues the designer must come to grips with.

THE HARDWARE ENVIRONMENT

Another consideration the designer has is the hardware environment in which the extract processing will be done. There are two possibilities:

- Both the original and the extracted data will reside on the same processor.
- The original data base will reside on one processor and the extracted data base will reside on another processor.

As long as there is only a modest amount of data and as long as there is only a small amount of processing being done, there is no reason why both the original data base and the extracted data base cannot reside on the same machine. But in the face of much data and/or much processing, it makes sense to split the data across separate machines.

In general, the original data will come from the operational, production environment. The extracted data will form the foundation for decision support processing. The generic patterns of processing are very different. Production processing usually entails a fairly static usage of machine resources, whereas decision support processing entails a dynamic, unpredictable usage of machine resources. Separating the two patterns of machine utilization in the face of volumes of processing makes sense.

When the original data base resides on a separate machine from the extracted data, there can be a beneficial separation of processing. The extract process is broken into two distinct operations: a selection and extract process (from the original file) and a load process (into the extracted file). The actual selection and extract processing takes place on the production machine. The data is then transferred to the machine where the extracted data will reside, and the load process is done there. In such a manner the CPU cycles from two machines share the workload. In addition, if there is a need for summarization or other refinement of data, the machine on which the extracted data resides can be used.

Separating extracted and original data over multiple machines has another beneficial effect. When the extract process is separated, there is a clarity of processing that does not exist if all extract processing is done on a single machine. When extract processing is done on a single machine, the code that supports the extract process may become entangled with regular application code. Once this happens, it is difficult to address the problems of extract processing independent of the application.

For example, a data base has been designed for an oil company to keep track of oil shipments on a daily basis as the shipments arrive. Billing, refinery, and allocation is done based on the values in the data base. In addition, an archiving of shipments is stored in the same data base. After a day's shipment is processed, the record of activity is kept in the same data base, but simply written into an archival portion. The archive of shipment records is used for decision support analysis, looking at historical trends, and so forth. Over time, however, the shipment data base grows, and the volume of processing overwhelms the machine. Attempting to remove the archival shipment processing from the application is a very disruptive thing to do.

Had the application been designed so that current-value shipment data would not be archived off into the same data base, managing the problems of volume at a later moment in time would have been much simpler. If, in the original design of the application, there had been a separate extract program that periodically examined shipment records for inclusion in a separate archival file, then the problems of volumes of data and consumption of I/O could have been dealt with separately. But trying to separate extract processing at a later point in time is awkward.

THE PIGGYBACK APPROACH

In truth, extract processing usually grows in an undisciplined fashion. But for those organizations that are facing a large amount of extract processing, a disciplined approach is in order.

Consider an undisciplined extract environment. On Day 1, an extract program is designed to look at a personnel file selecting all male employees. On Day 2, another extract program is written to look at employees who make more than $50,000 annually. On Day 3, a third extract is written to look at employees who have advanced college degrees. While none of the three extracts consumes too many resources by itself, collectively they consume a fair amount of resources.

The scan portion of the extract might be streamlined so that only one scan of the personnel data base needs to be done looking for data that fits one or more of the criteria that are being considered. The logic of the scan program determines if the record being examined is a male, makes more than $50,000 annually, or has an advanced college degree. The record is written to as many extract files as there are criteria that are satisfied. There is a wholesale waste of I/O in the scanning of the same personnel data base three times.

The discipline required for the "piggyback" approach mandates that not only current extract requirements be consolidated, but that all future requirements be consolidated as well. In other words, whenever a new extract requirement has been identified, the first step the designer takes is to determine what extracts already exist that can be used. The only time the designer specifies a new extract be written is if the extract is against a data base that has no extracts already going against it.

The savings in combining criteria to achieve a single scan of data shows up in the I/O needed for the first part of the extract process. Of course, multipurpose scans probably look at data on a record-by-record basis, rather than accessing data through the index.

There is a point at which scanning an entire data base rather than looking at data through the index becomes more efficient. When there are many rows of data that satisfy the search criteria, it is faster to sequentially scan the table than to access data through an index. When there are only a few rows that satisfy the selection criteria, it is more efficient to search tables through the index, since each row is most likely in a different page than the last row that satisfied the search criteria. If there are many pages that satisfy the search criteria, then many pages will need to be brought into memory.

INCREMENTAL CHANGES

Some extract processing consists of a blind copy of all data into the extracted format, in which case the extract appears to be a "snapshot" of data as of some moment in time. There may be large savings in this type of extract processing if only occurrences of data that have had changes since the last extract are selected for the transportation across the barrier to the extracted file.

As an example, suppose that in an Army personnel data base all officers have their active files extracted every six months into an archived format. This extract (which occurs two times a year) selects all Army officers and thus takes a long time because there are many officers.

Another approach is to select only officers who have undergone a change in status in the previous six months, which means many fewer officers could be selected for the extract. For example, if any of the following criteria are met, then the officer is selected for the extract:

- If marital status changed.
- If rank changed.

- If an advanced degree was obtained.
- If there was a change in dependents.
- If the officer received training in a new subject.

The selection of only a subset of data based on incremental activity saves processing in both the scan and the load portions of the extract process. Unfortunately, such an approach probably will require logic in the loading of the extracted data that otherwise would not have been needed. However, the additional logic and complexity are usually worth the savings in processing.

INDEXES AND EXTRACTED DATA

The amount of time required to load extracted data can quickly grow to an unreasonable level if there is a lot of data to be loaded and if the data to be loaded requires that one or more indexes be loaded at the same time. The designer should be *very careful* of large extracted files with multiple indexes. He or she should not take for granted that an index is needed for extracted data. Each index should be individually justified.

Certainly, clustering the extracted data can reduce the time and DASD required to load one index, but tables can be clustered only once. Clustering an extracted file thus has only limited applicability.

Another approach to managing large extracts of data and their corresponding large indexes is to break the extracted data into multiple separate tables. For example, suppose an insurance company annually extracts the history of claims that have been settled and/or received by the company. Each year the company receives a large number of claims.

The simplest approach is simply to load the extracted data into a table and create indexes. But the insurance company quickly discovers that the load and index building process takes an inordinate amount of time.

The designer then decides to break the claims table up into twelve categories. There will be a claims table not for the entire year's worth of claims, but for each month in the year. In other words, depending on when the claim was made, there will be a January claims table, a February claims table, a March claims table, and so forth. The resulting tables and their associated indexes take roughly one-twelfth of the time to load. Of course, the load process in total still takes as long to execute, but the load process is broken up into units that are much more amenable to normal operations. And there is the possibility of being able to execute the load processes in parallel.

Even though there is no real savings in the division of a table and its associated indexes into small components, there are real gains in the operability and usability of such data.

It is fair to question what the splitting of a table does to program logic that is required to access the table. Consider the request against the single large table of insurance claims:

```
SELECT DATE AMOUNT FROMNAME
FROM CLAIMS
WHERE CLAIMANT="Jackson, Bob'
```

When the table is divided, the same request must be run multiple times, as in the following:

```
SELECT DATE AMOUNT FROMNAME
FROM CLAIMJAN
WHERE CLAIMANT="Jackson, Bob'

SELECT DATE AMOUNT FROMNAME
FROM CLAIMFEB
WHERE CLAIMANT="Jackson, Bob'

SELECT DATE AMOUNT FROMNAME
FROM CLAIMMAR
WHERE CLAIMANT="Jackson, Bob'

SELECT DATE AMOUNT FROMNAME
FROM CLAIMAPR
WHERE CLAIMANT="Jackson, Bob'
 .   .   .   .   .   .   .   .   .   .
 .   .   .   .   .   .   .   .   .   .
 .   .   .   .   .   .   .   .   .   .
 .   .   .   .   .   .   .   .   .   .
 .   .   .   .   .   .   .   .   .   .
```

(Note: One SELECT using the UNION operator could have been used as well.)

At first glance the amount of work—both for development and maintenance—required of the programmer appears to have taken an enormous leap. But the requests are repetitious and can easily be generated or otherwise controlled automatically. In addition, there may well be some very important performance gains in the accessing of the tables that have been built, because each request of the claims data does not have to access the entire table.

When dealing with large tables where there are known requirements to access subsets of the data, it may make sense to create "sparse indexes." A sparse index in ORACLE is a construct created and supported entirely at the application level. The sparse index is most likely created as the extracted data is loaded.

As an example of the usage of a sparse index in conjunction with extracted data, consider a home mortgage financial institution with a data base that tracks payment activities. Once a month, the payment activities are extracted and put in an archival data base.

Most payments are made on time, and there is little to say about them. But occasionally a payment is late and a penalty is added. The decision support analyst has to track how many loans are late, whether the same loans are chronically late, and what the trend of late payments looks like over a five-year period.

One approach is to create an index for all loans that is loaded at the moment the extract data is loaded. Most loans have a penalty payment value of $0.00. But every loan has a late payment record each month. In short, there is a lot of index space that is wasted and a lot of time loading the index that has gone for naught.

The designer could have specified a separate table—a late payments table—to be loaded each month at the same time the extract data is loaded. The late payments table contains the identification of the loan that was late and the amount of the penalty. There would be (relatively speaking!) only a few loans in the late payments table, and an index could easily be created for it. Processing could go against the table for analysis of late payments, and, when needed, the individual late loans could be accessed using information from the late payments table.

The late payments table, then, serves as a separate adjunct to the regular monthly payments table.

The creation of a sparse index does not speed up the extract process. However, it does create the opportunity for efficient usage of extract data and possibly precludes the need for the loading of one or more indexes against a large table.

PERIODIC LOADING

Normally, extract processing is thought of as an activity that is run overnight or in a batch window. In normal circumstances, there is no opportunity to run extract processing during the online day.

However, on occasion an extract process can be broken up into fine components and run in the middle of the online day, and when those occasions arise, it may make sense to do so. In a sense, the extract processing becomes a "background" type of processing. Note that this option must be considered carefully and does not fit the general case for extract processing.

When an extract can be broken into fine pieces and when there are slack moments of online processing during the production day, then there may be an opportunity to schedule some of the extract processing during these slack moments.

Some of the conditions where this type of processing can be done are where:

- The extract program can "remember" where it last left off.
- No update activity will occur that will destroy the integrity of the extract.
- The extract program can be selectively scheduled.
- The extract program can be stopped and restarted gracefully.
- There is a production workload with a great deal of variability in the amount of processing power that is used.

The ability to run extract processing during the online day does not shorten or lengthen the total amount of resources spent for extract processing. Instead, the capability spreads the demand for resources over a wider time frame.

COMPACTING DATA

A very useful design technique for the minimization of resources in the load portion of the extract process is the physical compaction of data. When data can be compacted, less of it is used (saving DASD) and less processor capacity is required to retrieve it.

One of the best techniques for compacting data is the creation of arrays of data inside a row. This form of denormalization cannot be used as a general solution.

As an example of the proper usage of an array within a row,

consider a payroll history file. In this example, employees are paid twice a month. Periodically, the last few months of payroll activity are extracted and put onto a payroll history file. The data elements extracted include:

▪ Employee number	char(19)
▪ Social security number	char(9)
▪ Paydate—yrmoda	char(6)
▪ Gross amount	number(11,2)
▪ Net amount	number(11,2)
▪ FICA	number(9,2)
▪ State tax	number(9,2)
▪ Federal tax	number(9,2)
▪ Insurance	number(9,2)
▪ Other deductions	number(9,2)
	71 bytes

Each pay period is defined to be another occurrence in the extracted history table for payroll. The data is defined to be in an array so that repeating groups are combined under a single employee, as shown:

▪ Employee number	char(19)
▪ Social security number	char(9)
▪ Paydate—yr	char(2)
▪ Gross amount(1)	number(11,2)
▪ Net amount(1)	number(11,2)
▪ FICA(1)	number(9,2)
▪ State tax(1)	number(9,2)
▪ Federal tax(1)	number(9,2)
▪ Insurance(1)	number(9,2)
▪ Other deductions(1)	number(9,2)
▪ Gross amount(2)	number(11,2)
▪ Net amount(2)	number(11,2)
▪ FICA(2)	number(9,2)
▪ State tax(2)	number(9,2)
▪ Federal tax(2)	number(9,2)
▪ Insurance(2)	number(9,2)
▪ Other deductions(2)	number(9,2)
▪ Gross amount(3)	number(11,2)
▪ Net amount(3)	number(11,2)
▪ FICA(3)	number(9,2)

■ State tax(3)	number(9,2)
■ Federal tax(3)	number(9,2)
■ Insurance(3)	number(9,2)
■ Other deductions(3)	number(9,2)
■ Gross amount(4)	number(11,2)
■ Net amount(4)	number(11,2)
■ FICA(4)	number(9,2)
■ State tax(4)	number(9,2)
■ Federal tax(4)	number(9,2)
■ Insurance(4)	number(9,2)
■ Other deductions(4)	number(9,2)
....	
....	
....	
....	
....	
■ Gross amount(24)	number(11,2)
■ Net amount(24)	number(11,2)
■ FICA(24)	number(9,2)
■ State tax(24)	number(9,2)
■ Federal tax(24)	number(9,2)
■ Insurance(24)	number(9,2)
■ Other deductions(24)	number(9,2)
	938 bytes

By storing the payroll history data together in an array where the twice-monthly pay information can be stored for an employee, there is savings in both space and processing. Space is saved because there is less total data in the table and there is one-twenty fourth the amount of space needed for the index. Processing is saved because one I/O is all that is needed to gather the annual payroll history for an employee. In the case where each payroll entry is its own row, as much as 24 times as much I/O is required.

The practice of blocking data at the application level when suitable saves considerable processing not only for extract loads but for extract scans as well. If a designer is faced with an extract scan that promises to consume huge amounts of resources, he or she is advised to look into the blocking of data in the production data base.

A FINAL NOTE

Even though the following comment does not directly relate to the efficiency of the extract process, it is tangentially relevant. It is good practice to time stamp each extract. The time stamp can often be used to clarify exactly what data has and has not been extracted. By virtue of the fact that a well-designed time stamping scenario for each extract of data may save much unnecessary processing, time stamping is a sound design practice.

SUMMARY

Extract processing is a necessary part of the ORACLE production environment. Extract processing represents the fundamental transformation of data from a highly structured, operational environment to a more flexible, less structural dss environment.

Some of the salient issues of ORACLE extract processing are:

- The frequency of the extract
- The amount of data extracted
- The granularity of the data extracted
- The set of data extracted (to include as many processing requests as possible)

QUESTIONS: EXTRACT PROCESSING IN ORACLE

1. Extract processing logic is SIMPLE/COMPLEX.
2. The primary problem posed by extract processing lies in:
   a. the volume of data that must be processed
   b. the maintenance of code
   c. the machine resources used
   d. the flexibility of the extract process
   e. the volume of data and the machine resources used
3. Extract processing grows in a/an ______________ manner:
   a. orderly
   b. undisciplined
   c. sequenced
   d. random
   e. application-oriented

4. In addition to the amount of machine resources required, extract processing also consumes much ______________.
5. Extract processing in ORACLE is done by the ______________.
6. Extract processing knows what data to select because of the ______________ that are passed to it.
7. Extract processing usually selects data from ______________ sources(s)?
8. Extract processing may proceed sequentially through a data base or may make use of an ______________.
9. After data is selected by the extract program, it is transported to the ______________.
10. The output file may be in the same format as the original data, or the output file may be ______________, ______________ or otherwise altered.
11. Some of the uses of the extract file are ______________, ______________, ______________.
12. The extract of data represents a major ______________ of data.
13. In some cases, the ultimate use and disposition of extracted data is well known. (T/F)
14. When the requirements for extracted data are well known there SHOULD/SHOULD NOT be any data extracted that will not be used.
15. When the requirements for extracted data are not well defined, there SHOULD/SHOULD NOT be any data extracted that may not be needed.
16. Anticipating requirements even where requirements are ambiguous IS/IS NOT a worthwhile practice.
17. Data that will not be needed should be stored on a ______________ medium.
18. Restoring data from a bulk medium is ______________.
19. Storing more data than is needed in the face of unknown requirements is ______________.
20. Granularity of data refers to the level of ______________ of the rows of data.
21. The most granular data in the system is always located at the store of data that is being ______________.
22. Upon extraction, rows of data may be ______________.

23. The ______________ level of detail that satisfies the usage of the extracted data should be chosen.

24. The data elements chosen for extraction depend upon the ultimate ______________ of the elements.

25. The weeding out of data elements DOES/DOES NOT save scan processing.

26. The weeding out of data elements DOES/DOES NOT save load processing.

27. The extracted data and the original data may reside on the same machine if there is ______________ of data.

28. When there is a lot of data, it is a good design practice to ______________ the data off onto two or more processors.

29. The extract process can be broken into two distinct sets of activities—a ______________ process and a ______________ process.

30. When the extract process is split over two processors, the ______________ cycles are divided.

31. One way to minimize scan time is to ______________ search criterion into a single program so that one pass of data is required.

32. All new extract requirements should first be analyzed to determine whether they can be "piggybacked" onto an existing extract. (T/F)

33. Piggyback scans of data that service multiple search criteria of necessity must ______________ search each row.

34. All data can be extracted at once, or only data that has ______________ since the last extract may be extracted.

35. It is almost always MORE/LESS efficient to extract only data that has changed since the last extract.

36. It is almost always MORE/LESS complicated to extract only data that has changed since the last extract.

37. Indexing extracted data is AN IMPORTANT/ A TRIVIAL issue.

38. Extracted data requires ______________ in order to be processed efficiently.

39. Each index requires ______________ and ______________ at the time of loading.

40. The size of the tables being loaded may be broken into finer levels at the ______________ or the ______________ level.

41. Breaking data into partitions DOES/DOES NOT reduce the time required for an individual load program that operates on an individual partition.
42. Breaking data into partitions simplifies the job of the programmer (T/F)
43. A sparse index is created at the ______________ level.
44. A sparse index can greatly REDUCE/INCREASE the size of the index into a large extracted table.
45. A sparse index INCREASES/DECREASES the total amount of DASD required.
46. Extract processing is always done overnight or during the batch window (T/F)
47. Extract processing may be able to be done during the online day. (T/F)
48. When extract processing is done during the day, it is run as a ______________ process.
49. When extract processing is done during the online day, it is done in a series of ______________ bursts.
50. Compacting data reduces load time in that less ______________ is required to load data.
51. Creating arrays of data in a row is a common form of compaction. This design technique can be done only under stringent conditions. (T/F)
52. Creating arrays of data HAS NO EFFECT ON/REDUCES DRAMATICALLY the index space required.
53. Creating arrays of data IMPLIES/DOES NOT IMPLY that individual occurrences of data can be accessed directly.
54. When there are a variable number of occurrences of data per row, creating internal arrays of data SHOULD/SHOULD NOT be done.
55. The frequency of extract processing IS/IS NOT a variable at which the designer should look.

CHAPTER 11

Testing ORACLE Production Systems

This discussion is divided into two sections. the first discusses the establishment and usage of the ORACLE test environment. It is for the data base administrator, the system administrator, or anyone interested in the ORACLE testing environment. The second is on testing individual ORACLE programs, primarily for the production environment. This section is for programmers.

I. The ORACLE Test Environment

ORACLE is a powerful tool that can be used in many different ways. When it is used in the ad hoc or information center environment, there is a need to test the accuracy of programs so that the proper calculations are done. But when it is used in the production mode, there is a need to do much more rigorous testing because there are more variables to account for. Not only is the testing of code and algorithms important in the production environment, so too are the usage of data, the volume of processing, the volume of data, and so forth. By the time an application goes into implementation, it is expensive to try to retrofit characteristics such as performance and availability into the production environment. Properly executed testing, then, is one of the major keys to the achievement of satisfactory ORACLE production systems. Of course, testing should be done not only for new development, but for changes to existing systems as well.

The first step in the proper testing of an ORACLE application is the establishment of the test environment.

There are three major components to the ORACLE test environment: the input used to drive the test environment, the data bases on which testing is done, and the actual configuration of the software controlling interaction with terminals (sometimes referred to as the "teleprocessing monitor") and ORACLE. Each of these components will be discussed at length.

INPUT TO TESTING

Input to the test environment is what is used to stimulate the execution of ORACLE transactions and programs. As in any test environment, the input needs to be carefully constructed in order to fully verify the many conditions that may occur once the system is into production. Typically, test input must be carefully coordinated with test data so that nonsensical conditions will not arise. For example, an update of a table where no rows exist serves only to check out exception logic —the test does not check out the actual application update logic. Because of the need to orchestrate input and test data carefully, care should be taken in the design, execution, and ultimate storage of both test input and test data.

Input test data serves at least two purposes: the verification of program logic and the means to "stress" test the system. There are different considerations to both types of testing. The testing of program logic should test all reasonable possible conditions, both legitimate and illegitimate. Illegitimate conditions should trigger error conditions and should be handled without bringing the system down. Legitimate input should exercise the full cycle of data—from creation to deletion. Of course, the interrelationships of ORACLE tables should be tested as well.

The testing of programmatic relationships usually requires that each unit of input be created manually in coordination with a known test data base. To verify that inserts, deletes, etc., are being done properly requires a foreknowledge of what data is and is not in the test data base. Because of the complexity of the conditions that may exist and the need for coordination between data and program, the data for the testing of programmatic relationships is usually small. The test data base, of course, must be able to be reinitialized to recreate the test conditions.

STRESS TESTS

Stress tests of an ORACLE application are not nearly as sensitive to program logic that is being executed. The essence of the stress test is not to verify the program logic, but to determine what resources are being used. Indeed, the same activity can often be run repeatedly in a stress test. However, stress tests are sensitive to the amount of data, the amount of activity, and the rate at which the activity arrives that will be executed in the production environment.

As long as the mixture of updates to access is properly maintained, as long as the sequence of transactions is properly constructed, and as long as the jobstream being used for testing is representative of the final implemented workload and does not create queues that would not naturally form otherwise, practically any transaction will do for stress testing of an ORACLE application.

For systems that are being converted rather than written for the first time, a sampling of existing transactions may suffice as input into the stress test. Of course, when existing transactions are used for stress testing, care must be taken not to update or transact against real data. For new applications, the input for stress testing must be created from scatch.

Stress Testing and Service-Level Agreements

In some cases, the maximum number of transactions that must be driven through the online system is known. The stress test must then achieve the same level of throughput to simulate the workload that will be implemented. In the case where the maximum workload is known, it is good practice to drive the system at least 10 percent higher than the maximum known rate of transaction processing. This slight overkill may be useful in identifying "hot spots" in the design and represents some degree of protection if the maximum rate that is targeted is too low. In the case where the maximum transaction rate is not known, it is good practice to estimate as carefully as possible the maximum transaction arrival rate and then add 25 percent for the purposes of testing.

Of course, the maximum transaction arrival rate used for stress testing represents *all* the transactions that will be flowing through the system during peak-period production processing.

In ORACLE, not only must the maximum transaction arrival rate be taken into consideration, but the actual number of I/Os done by the transactions must be accounted for also. Because ORACLE does set-at-a-time processing, it is possible to have a wide variation in the resources used by different transactions or even by the same transaction operating on different data. For example, at one point in time ORACLE may be servicing transactions at a rate of 25 per second. But because the transactions are accessing only very small sets of data, only 100 I/Os per second are being serviced by ORACLE at that time.

At a later point in time, ORACLE is servicing 15 transactions per second, but the transactions are accessing very large sets of data. At this point in time, ORACLE is servicing 200 I/Os per second. In this case, the maximum transaction arrival rate is misleading. A better measurement is the total activity being done by ORACLE, such as the number of pages being accessed per unit of time.

Measuring the Stress Test

The result of the stress test is measured in two ways: by the ORACLE data base monitor and by measurement of the flow through the teleprocessing monitor or the software that controls the flow of activity to and from the terminal and the computer. Monitoring the data base helps to locate the data bases that were stressed during the test and to locate any bottlenecks or potential bottlenecks.

The measurement of activity run through the teleprocessing monitor gives information about response time, arrival rates, queue lengths, and so forth. For example, suppose that ORACLE is running in MVS and is fed transactions by CICS. The CICS trace facility will yield the desired results needed to measure the terminal activity through the system at the moment of highest stress. In the ORACLE production environment, information about *both* data base and teleprocessor activities are necessary for evaluating the results of stress testing.

Another type of stress test that needs to be run for ORACLE production systems is the determination of the length of the batch window requirements. Of course, the batch window must be long enough for the entire stream of batch processes to run.

Estimating batch run time is a fairly straightforward process. The first calculation is to determine the ratio of the size of the test data base versus the size of the production data base. A ratio of 1:5, for example, indicates that the test data base is about one-fifth the size of the production data base. In general, a ratio of 1:10 or less may produce faulty results because of anomalies that arise with batch startup and shutdown time. As a rule, any data base ratio less than 1:10 should not be used for batch stress testing.

After the ratio is determined, the length of the test run is measured by the reciprocal of the ratio. If the ratio is 1:5 and the length of the batch test run is 3 minutes and 30 seconds (or 210 seconds) then:

$$210 \times 5 = 1050 \text{ seconds} = 17.5 \text{ minutes}$$

All batch processing to be run in the batch window must be accumulated to determine whether the batch window will be adequate.

This rough extrapolation process to determine the length of time required for batch processing serves as a fairly accurate guideline as long as the batch process is not doing many relational joins. If the batch process is doing a fair amount of relational joins, it is recommended that a ratio of no less than 1:3 be used. The resources required for relational joins oftentimes do not occur in an arithmetic progression and tend to skew a simple extrapolation method as has been described.

DRIVER PROGRAMS

Input used to test program logic is usually run through a driver. A driver program is one that simply reads the input, translates it into a transaction, and then issues the transaction to the teleprocessing monitor. Of course, if the instance is not equipped with a teleprocessing monitor, the transaction goes directly to the ORACLE kernel.

Oftentimes when stress testing is done, the driver program is a standard piece of software that feeds transactions to the teleprocessing monitor (if equipped).

When testing occurs in the teleprocessing environment, such as the CICS environment, it usually is done on a separate system that is running another copy of CICS specially designated for testing.

Modularized Programs

On occasion, a program will be modularized so that the teleprocessing activity is separated from the data base activity within the application program.

SEPARATE ENVIRONMENTS

Only under very unusual circumstances will the test environment actually be the same as the production environment. If the organization is embarking on its very first application, there may be ample resources available to actually test in the production environment. But once the production environment begins to operate on live data and execute real programs and transactions, computing resources become taxed to the point that testing and production processing cannot gracefully coexist in the same environment.

In addition, when testing is done in the production environment, there is always the possibility that it will cause errors that will show up in production processing—potentially costing performance and availability.

Another powerful motivation for separating the test and the production environment is to enable new software release testing to be done in the test environment without disturbing the production environment.

"PRELIMINARY" AND "FULL" TEST DATA BASES

In the ORACLE test environment, two types of test data bases are required. One—the "preliminary" test data base (or baseline test data base) is used to check program logic. It is small and contains only the minimum data needed to verify that a program is operable. Generally speaking, this ORACLE test data base can be altered at will by the programmers testing on it, and it may be reinitialized as often as necessary. The preliminary test data base represents the organization "in miniature."

One of the unique uses of the preliminary test data base is as a basis for testing sequences of transactions. Often, transactions are designed so that they execute in a prescribed sequence. Testing the sequence of execution is easy with the preliminary test data base because it is small enough to be easily reinitialized each time the sequence of the transactions needs to be repeated.

The second type of data base needed in the ORACLE environment is the "full" test data base. The full test data base should be no less than 10 percent of the size of the final implemented production data base, and it should contain one set of every variety that will need to be tested. In addition, the *maximum* set size should be included for each set. Under most circumstances, it is not a trivial exercise to accurately create the maximum set size that is needed in the full test data base. It is not normal to reinitialize the full test data base frequently due to its size.

The full test data base must contain at least one occurrence of the maximum set size of each set that will be accessed because of the set processing nature of SQL.

When ORACLE testing is done on only small sets, the full impact of production data is hard to gauge. In the test environment, where a test operates on small sets of data, a transaction may appear not to consume many resources, but when the same transaction—using the same programming logic—runs in the production environment, it consumes many more resources because it operates on much larger data bases that contain much larger sets of data. A program in the test environment that runs in 2 to 3 seconds may execute in 35 to 45 seconds in the production environment. The difference in the execution of the program in the test and the production environments is in the set size on which the program operates. And the set size dissimilarities make a *huge* difference in the amount of resources used in execution.

If there is going to be a problem with large variations in set sizes between the test and the production environments, the problem needs to be discovered in testing. The only way to do this is to create maximum set sizes in the full test data base. Therefore, the full test ORACLE environment must be created carefully.

The difference between the full test and the preliminary test environments is in day-to-day usage. The preliminary test data base is merely for simple, quick tests. As a programmer creates new modules, iterative tests are run against the preliminary test data base. Mistakes and errors arise very frequently in the preliminary environment and are expected, but the size and general usage of the preliminary test data are such that errors are tolerated. The preliminary test data base is much like a "scratch pad" or a work area data base.

The full test data base environment is used much less frequently than the preliminary test environment. After a program has been shaken out and the first iterations of testing against the preliminary data base have been completed, testing against the full test data base can commence.

TESTING COORDINATION ACROSS PROJECTS

One of the knotty issues of testing ORACLE applications is the coordination of testing across the different parties involved in development. In a large project, the issues of coordination of testing can be very complex. One solution is to give each project its own small test data base to test against, after which the project tests against a larger, community data base.

This approach has the advantage of keeping people from stepping on each other's toes at the inception of the project. However, it requires the establishment of *many* test data bases, which can be a burdensome task. In addition, once the project begins to maintain and alter its own project data, there tends to be very little coordination of test results with other projects.

Another approach is to establish community preliminary and community full test data bases. This approach is simpler and requires fewer resources. But it requires greater coordination between projects as one project and then another accesses and manipulates the community data.

Creating a test log identifying changes to a data base made by a given test is one technique for interproject coordination between data bases. The log contains the date of the test, who conducted the test, and what data was altered, and is updated each time a test is made.

The log can be kept externally with a simple pad of paper, or it can be formalized as an actual part of the test data base and actually updated as part of the test. Logging of alterations of the data base can be done at the row or even the field level if necessary. The log is useful in determining exactly what tests have been done and when. For example, if a programmer looks today for data that was there yesterday and does not find it, he or she can look to the log to explain why unexpected results occur.

ADMINISTERING THE TEST ENVIRONMENT

The ORACLE test environment must be managed just like any other data base environment. It is a task that usually falls to the data base administrator. The data base administrator is responsible for, among other things:

- Creating tables
- Granting, revoking authority
- Creating, restoring utilities
- Monitoring size and content of test data bases
- Moving table definitions from test to production
- Monitoring, administering naming conventions

Generally speaking, the test environment requires much less attention than does the production environment. Only during peak periods of testing will the test environment consume the attention of the data base administrator.

One of the important issues of administering the test environment is who is in charge of creating/altering test data bases. Unlike in the production environment, where data base alterations are done infrequently and under careful control, in the test environment data structures change frequently.

The data base administrator may become a roadblock for progress if he or she enforces very tight data base administration controls in the test environment. While there are no concrete rules that apply to determine where the data base administrator should and should not have control, the following guidelines may be used:

DBA control—
- –large projects
- –projects requiring control over different development groups
- –projects involving large data bases
- –projects where reinitialization of test data bases is done frequently
- –projects where development will occur over a long period of time
- –projects for operational systems
- –projects built under a data architecture

Application control—
- –small projects
- –projects with a very tight deadline
- –decision support projects
- –departmental projects
- –projects independent of other development groups
- –projects that have no future development planned
- –projects that do not involve high performance
- –projects dealing with summarized data
- –projects dealing with subsets of data

Whatever stance taken by the organization, it should be clear at the outset of the project who will be controlling the data base creation and manipulation. It is a mistake to take a *laissez faire* approach and let the ambiguities of control be resolved by default.

SUMMARY

This section has discussed the importance of the test environment and three aspects that are essential to it: the input to testing, the data bases on which testing is done, and the actual physical environment.

There are two types of test to be done for the production environment: programmatic tests, which verify program logic, and stress tests, which verify that the volume of data and processing to be run in production will not overwhelm the resources available. Two types of data bases are recommended: a "preliminary" test data base and a "full" data base.

The results of the stress test can be measured in several ways: by the teleprocessing monitor, by a data base monitor, or programmatically.

Driver programs are a necessary part of the test environment. They may be written at the application level or may be a standard piece of software.

Separate environments are necessary for a variety of reasons, such as the resources consumed by the production environment and the chance that the production environment may actually be modified by testing.

II. Testing Programs in ORACLE

The first step in program testing in ORACLE is the verification of program logic validity. If program logic is not correct, then very little else matters. To verify program logic in ORACLE requires test tables, the contents of which directly affect the success or validity of the test. The programmer must carefully predetermine what data is or is not present in the test data base prior to the test.

Because of the need to closely coordinate program testing with the contents of the test data base, the programmer often must reinitialize the test data base prior to execution. Reinitialization ensures that if other tests have been executed against the test data base, the contents of the test data base are in a known state. There are standard reinitialization routines available to reset the test data base. The data base administrator or the project manager will be able to point out what these routines are.

After the test data base has been reinitialized, the program test may commence. The test is run in the teleprocessing monitoring environment (if applicable) where testing is set up. Sometimes program tests consist of running a single program; other times a test requires that several transactions or programs be run in sequence. When one transaction alters a table and another transaction enters the same table and accesses the data that has been altered by the first transaction, then the transactions must be sequenced together.

Actual transactions may be fed to the test system in sequence or parameters may be consecutively passed to a driver program that, in turn, uses the parameters for the creation of transactions. After the driver program has created the transaction, the transaction is fed to the test system for execution.

On occasion, it may be necessary to put special instructions in the test version of a program to aid in debugging the program. These special instructions help trace the logic and the sequence of execution of the program. Upon completion of testing, these special instructions are removed, and, at that point, it is good practice to retest the programs.

After the execution of the transaction or transactions, the results of the test are verified through a variety of channels such as application traces, dumps of the test data base, screen transmissions, or reports. The programmatic conditions that should be checked include the following.

GENERAL TRANSACTION/PROGRAM CONTROL

- Input all parameters that are valid.
- Input combinations of valid and invalid parameters.
- Input less than all parameters needed.
- (If possible) Input more than valid parameters.
- Identify and cause to execute ALL abnormal ending conditions:
  –repair from dump, if dump occurs,
  –repair data base, if data base goes down,
  –repair transaction definition to tp monitor, if damaged.

SINGLE TABLE MANIPULATION

- Insert against a row that already exists.
- Insert against a row that does not exist.
- Delete a row that does not exist.
- Delete a row that does exist.
- Update a row that does exist.
- Update a row that does not exist.
- Insert a row so that null values are created.
- Insert a row with values in range of edits.
- Insert a row with values out of edit range.

- Update a row with values in range of edits.
- Update a row with values out of edit range.
- Where there is a relationship between two or more fields in the same row:
  –create a change in row A, observe the effect on other variables,
  –create a change in row A which is invalid, observe the effect on other related variables.

REFERENTIAL INTEGRITY

- Where row B can exist only when row A exists:
  –attempt to create row B when row A does not exist,
  –attempt to create row B where row A does exist.
- Where row B is deleted when row A is deleted:
  –attempt to delete row A and not delete row B,
  –attempt to delete row A and delete row B as well.
- Where row A and row B may exist independently but where there may be a relationship between the two:
  –create row A and row B independently,
  –create a relationship between row A and row B where both exist,
  –attempt to create a relationship between row A and row B where row A does not exist,
  –attempt to create a relationship between row A and row B where row B does not exist,
  –attempt to delete row A where a relationship has been already established,
  –attempt to delete row B where a relationship has already been established,
  –delete the relationship between row A and row B,
  –change the relationship between row A and row B to a relationship between row A and row C,
  –in the case where separate relationships between row A and row B and row B and row A are kept (i.e., A/B and B/A are maintained):
    –change A/B and observe the effect on B/A,
    –delete A/B and observe the effect on B/A,
    –insert A/B and observe the effect on B/A.

PROGRAM MODULARIZATION

- Determine what parameters are passed to each module:
  –pass more parameters than are necessary,

–pass less parameters than are necessary,
–pass invalid parameters,
–pass parameters in an invalid order.

- Determine what range any given parameter should have:
  –pass a value in the valid range,
  –pass a parameter out of the valid range,
- When an error condition is encountered in the called module, how does the calling module react?
- Create parameters that will cause each path of logic to be executed.
- what return codes from ORACLE are possible? will program logic handle all possible return codes?
  –create conditions that will simulate each ORACLE return code that is possible.
- Is there a standard module for the handling of errors?
- is there a standard module for the handling of calls to the data base (i.e., an I/O module)?
  –will the I/O module handle all needed conditions?

ALGORITHMIC VERIFICATION

- create input to exercise all algorithms:
  –verify the results of the calculation.

DATA ACCESS

- Access and display a row of data that is known to exist.
- Access and display a row of data that does not exist.
- Access a set of data that is known to exist.
- Access a set of data that does not exist.
- Access a set of data through all VIEWS that have been defined.

RECURSIVE RELATIONSHIPS

- When row A and row B are involved in a recursive relationship and row A exists in a superior relationship to row B:
  –insert row B without making row B subordinate to row A,
  –insert row B making row B subordinate to row A, when row A and row B exist:
  –attempt to delete row A without deleting the relationship to row B,

–delete row A and delete the relationship to row B,
–attempt to delete row B without deleting the relationship to row B,
–delete row B and the relationship to row A,
–insert row C as a subordinate of row A.

- For an explosion of the recursive relationship:
  –attempt to create an infinite relationship by creating the rows and relationships—row A → row B → row A → row B . . .
  –verify from program logic that the infinite loop has been detected.
- For dependents of a superior row where the dependents must be sequenced:
  –attempt to delete the first dependent row.
  –insert a dependent row at the last of the sequence.
  –attempt to insert a row in the middle of a consecutively ordered sequence of dependent rows.

CONTINUOUS TIME-SPAN ROWS

(where rows are logically grouped to form continuous definition of a variable)

- Insert a row at the start of the time span.
- Insert a row at the end of the time span.
- Update the variable for an amount of time completely contained within a single time span.
- Update the variable for an amount of time spanning more than one time span.
- Attempt to delete the variable for a period of time within the range of continuity.
- Delete all related time-span rows.
- Determine if two or more consecutive time spans can hold the same values for the variable—if so, why aren't the spans collapsed into a single row?

EXTRACT PROCESSING

- For the running of an extract program:
  –verify that all data that should be selected in fact is selected,
  –verify that no data that should not be selected in fact is not selected.

- For data that is accumulated, aggregated, etc., during extract:
  –verify that all data that should be aggregated in fact is aggregated,
  –verify that no data that should not be aggregated is in fact aggregated.
- Verify that the time and/or conditions of extract processing are able to be determined for each extract.

After programmatic testing is done, the next phase is stress testing.

When errors occur, there are a variety of sources to turn to for information on the resolution of the error. The most appropriate source is dependent on where the error was detected. A standard list of sources for error detection and diagnosis includes:

- Output from the precompiler, if a precompiler was used.
- Output from the compiler or assembler.
- Linkage editor output.
- Source listings of the program.
- System control used during execution.
- Application program output.
- System dumps.
- Data base or teleprocessing monitor of activity during execution.

Stress testing begins with identification of the full test data base. Generally, this data base will be different from the one under which the programmatic tests are run. The full test data base is a large data base that contains samples of the production data base that is to be built.

The point of testing against the full test data base is to determine how many resources are used by each of the processes that will be run.

A simple way the resources used in execution against the full test data base may be measured is by using a host variable to count each of the rows returned. The counter is initialized to zero, then, as each cursor positioning occurs, the host variable is incremented by one.

The results of the calculation may be displayed along with other data. When the host variable indicates that more than 75 total rows are accessed (note: this number is subject to variation if clustered data is being accessed), then the designer may want to consider alternate programming techniques. Of course, the display of the host variable is disabled upon going into production. The test and calculation of resources used against the full data base is especially important where relational joins are specified because of the potential resources that may be consumed by the join.

The final step in the stress test is the analysis of the arrival rate of the transactions. The anticipated arrival rate—at peak-period processing—is estimated. Next the transaction to be tested is aggregated with all other transactions that will be running during peak period and a test run is executed. Usually, the final stress test is administered by the data base administrator or the project manager who has overall project responsibility.

SUMMARY

The first step in testing is to select the test data base. This will usually be a prepared data base that contains data that can be tested against. The test data base needs to be reinitialized before each test to ensure that tests run since the last initialization have not altered the content of the data.

The first tests that are run address the algorithmic content of programs—is the program logic written correctly? Algorithmic verification is done in the following areas:

- General transaction/program control
- Single table manipulation
- Referential integrity
- Program modularization
- Algorithmic/calculation verification
- Data access
- Recursive relationships
- Continuous time-span creation/manipulation
- Extract processing

After programmatic testing comes stress testing. Stress testing is done against a data base specially designed just for it. The first part of stress testing determines how much data any given SQL call requires. If too much data is needed by a transaction, then the program must be broken into smaller pieces.

The final phase of testing is transaction arrival rate testing, where all transactions that will be run during peak periods are run together, simulating peak-period processing.

QUESTIONS: TESTING ORACLE PRODUCTION SYSTEMS

Section I

1. Testing IS/IS NOT important in the information center environment.
2. Testing is of MORE/LESS/EQUAL importance in the operational environment in relation to the ad hoc or information center environment.
3. In the production environment, two of the aspects of the design that must be tested are ______________ and ______________.
4. Even though an application has gone into production, tuning can be done to achieve online performance. (T/F)
5. Testing should be done for both ______________ systems and changes to ______________ systems.
6. The three components of the test environment are ______________, ______________, and ______________.
7. Test input MUST BE/SHOULD BE/MIGHT BE/SOMETIMES IS coordinated with test data in order to produce a meaningful test.
8. Input test data serves to verify program logic and to ______________ the system.
9. ALL/SOME/MOST program logic conditions should be tested.
10. An illegitimate condition should be detected without ______________ the system down.
11. Table ______________ should be tested in addition to program logic.
12. Testing programmatic relationships is done against LARGE/SMALL data bases.
13. When testing of programmatic relationships is done, the test data base is usually ______________ to ensure the status of the data.
14. Stress tests ARE/ARE NOT sensitive to program logic as a rule.
15. Stress tests are sensitive to: (pick all that apply)
    a. the rate of arrival of transactions
    b. the volume of data run against the data base during the test
    c. the language the program is written in
    d. the structure of the data run against
    e. the amount of processing done by the programmer

16. For conversions, existing transactions MAY/MAY NOT be used for input into the stress test.

17. When existing transactions are used for stress testing, care must be taken not to ________.

18. For new applications, test input must be ________.

19. When the number of transactions to flow through the system is known, it is good practice to stress the system at ________ more than the known rate.

20. Overstressing the system helps to identify ________.

21. In the case where the maximum flow through the system is not known, an estimate of the maximum rate is still important. (T/F)

22. In the case where the maximum flow through the system is not known, an estimate is made and the system is stressed at at least ________ more than the estimate.

23. The maximum rate that is stressed includes only the most important transactions that will be running through the system at the maximum moment of processing. (T/F)

24. Not only must stress testing account for the transaction arrival rate, but it must also account for the ________ done by the transaction.

25. The nature of ORACLE processing is RECORD-AT-A-TIME / SET-AT-A-TIME.

26. Because ORACLE does set-at-a-time processing, the amount of I/O done by a given transaction is highly ________.

27. The stress test should account for the ________ activity being done by the transaction, including I/O and data base calls.

28. The stress test is measured in the ________ and the ________.

29. Typical activity measured through the TP monitor is ________, ________, and ________.

30. Stress testing SHOULD/SHOULD NOT include estimates of the length of the batch window.

31. The batch window should be estimated for: (pick all that apply)

a. the peak period
b. the average day
c. a slack day
d. end-of-year processing
e. end-of-month processing

32. The "full" test data base should be no less than ______________ of the production data base.

33. Raw extrapolation of test to production runs based on data base size MAY/PROBABLY WILL NOT/WILL PROBABLY produce anomalies.

34. Raw extrapolation will most likely fail to account for initiation and ______________ times.

35. Batch testing in the face of many or large relational ______________ must be done very carefully.

36. The resources used for relational joins do not progress ______________ ; therefore extrapolations must be done carefully.

37. A driver program's prime purpose is to ______________ transactions.

38. The driver program is often a standard piece of software such as ______________ or ______________.

39. When testing is done in the production environment, there is always the possibility of ______________ live data and transactions.

40. ______________ types of data bases are required for testing in ORACLE.

41. One type of data base is the "full" data base; the other is the ______________ test data base.

42. The preliminary test data base is used to test ______________.

43. Because of its size, the preliminary test data base can be ______________.

44. The full test data base should be no smaller than ______________ of the production data base.

45. The full test data base should contain at least ______________ of every variety that will be encountered in the production data base.

46. It IS/IS NOT an easy exercise to properly create the full test data base environment.

47. Because of its size, the full test data base MAY/MAY NOT be easily reinitialized.

48. Because of the ______________ processing nature of SQL, the full test data base must contain one full set of every variety that will be encountered.

49. Because of the set processing nature of SQL, a transaction that runs in 2 to 3 seconds in the test environment may run in ______________ seconds in the production environment.
50. The problems in the variation of processing from the test to the production environment SHOULD/DO NOT NEED TO be discovered during testing.
51. The way to discover wide variations between testing and production processing is to create ______________ set sizes in the test environment.
52. The ______________ test data base environment is like a "scratch pad" or a work area data base.
53. In a large project each development group may have its own test data base. (T/F)
54. After doing preliminary testing against the "local" test data base, the project then does testing against the ______________ test data base.
55. Giving each development group its own test data base in a large project ultimately means that ______________ test data bases must be created.
56. A means of coordinating testing is through a ______________.
57. The test log contains such information as ______________, ______________, and ______________.
58. Five tasks that are in the domain of the data base administrator are ______________, ______________, ______________, ______________, and ______________.

Section II

1. The content of test data bases AFFECTS/DOES NOT AFFECT the validity of a test.
2. The programmer must ______________ what data is or is not present in the test data base prior to the test.
3. It is normal practice to ______________ a data base prior to testing.
4. The ______________ is able to point out what reinitialization routines are available.
5. Some tests require that a single program be run; other tests require the running of ______________ programs in sequence.

6. Actual transactions or transactions from a ______________ program may be used for the test.
7. Special debugging instructions MAY/MAY NOT be put into a program for testing.
8. The programmer must remember to ______________ the special debugging instructions before going into production.
9. Special debugging statements help to trace the ______________ of logic.
10. Five ways the results of the test can be verified are ______________, ______________, ______________, ______________, and ______________.
11. Transaction/program control testing ensures the ______________ of logic are correct.
12. All possible paths should be tested. (T/F)
13. Invalid data SHOULD/SHOULD NOT be used for transaction/program control testing.
14. ALL combinations of parameters, internal and external, should be tested. (T/F)
15. The programmer needs to ______________ the system to create abnormal return codes that can be returned by ORACLE.
16. Testing recovery routines is not important since the test data base can easily be reinitialized. (T/F)
17. Single table manipulation requires that an insert, a ______________, an ______________, and an access be done against a row.
18. Activity should be done against rows that exist and rows that do not exist, even though error conditions will be triggered. (T/F)
19. Insertion and updates of values in and out of ______________ should be done against single rows as well.
20. Where rows are related by means of a foreign key, the relationship is termed ______________.
21. Where row B exists only when row A exists, test logic should insert row B both when row A exists and when row A does not exist. (T/F)
22. Where row B is deleted, row B should be inserted before row A. (T/F)
23. Where there is an m:n relationship between row A and row B,

_____________ existence of the rows and the relationship should be verified during testing.

24. The issue of program modularization is NO MORE/NO LESS/ THE SAME in ORACLE as in regular systems.
25. Centralization of access to the data base is often done by means of an _____________.
26. Much code can be saved and responses can be standardized for incorrect conditions by means of an _____________.
27. Each error condition that can exist must be created by test conditions or by _____________.
28. All set sizes and all _____________ relationships must be verified by the I/O module.
29. A relationship of one type of data with itself is called a _____________ relationship.
30. Where row A is subordinate to row B, row B CANNOT/CAN/ MAY BE ABLE TO exist when row A does not exist.
31. The testing done for an infinite loop in a recursive relationship MAY/MAY NOT be removed from the program once the system is debugged.
32. Testing for data fracturing may be removed once continuous time updates and inserts are debugged. (T/F)
33. Five common sources of debugging information are _____________, _____________, _____________, _____________, and _____________.
34. After program logic is tested, then _____________ testing must be done.
35. Stress testing is run against the _____________ test data base.
36. The test administrator is usually responsible for coordinating the stress test of _____________ programs.
37. The purpose of the stress test is not to verify logic but to determine _____________ are used by the program.
38. Host variables may be used to count how many resources are used. Host variables must be _____________ by the program.
39. Relational _____________ cause special concern in testing because of the potential for using resources.

References

Astrahan, M., et al. (1979). "System R: Relational Approach to Database Management," IEEE Computer Society: *Computer* 12(5), May.

Chen P. (1977). *The Entity-Relationship Approach to Logical Data Base Design*, Data Base Monograph Series, N 6. Wellesley Mass.: QED Information Sciences, Inc.

Codd E.F. (1971). "Normalized Data Base Structures: A Brief Tutorial," *Proc. ACM SIGFIDET Workshop on Data Description, Access and Control.*

Date C.J. (1974). *An Introduction to Data Base Systems*, Addison-Wesley, Reading Mass.

Fagin, R. (1979). "Normal Forms And Relational Database Operators," *Proc. ACM SIGMOD International Conference on Management of Data.*

Inmon, W.H. (1989). *Data Architecture: The Information Paradigm*, QED Information Sciences, Inc., Wellesley, Mass.

———. (1987). *Information Engineering for the Practitioner*, Yourdon Press, New York.

———. (1986). *Information Systems Architecture*, Prentice-Hall, Englewood Cliffs, N.J.

———. (1984). "What Price Relational?," *ComputerWorld*, Nov.

———. (1980). *Effective Data Base Design*, Prentice-Hall, Englewood Cliffs, N.J.

Inmon, W.H. and Bird, T.J. (1986). *Dynamics of Data Base*, Prentice-Hall, Englewood Cliffs, N.J.

James, M. and Won, B. (1983). "Performance Management of Relational Database Systems," *Infoims*, 3rd quarter.

James, M. and Won, B. (1983). "Performance Management of Relational Database Systems," *Infoims*, 3rd quarter.

———. (1983). "Performance Management of Relational Database Systems—Part 2," *Infoims*, 4th quarter.

Kroenke, D. (1977). *Database Processing: Fundamentals, Modeling, Applications*, Science Research Associates, Palo Alto, Calif.

Martin, J. (1975). *Computer Data-Base Organization*, Prentice-Hall, Englewood Cliffs, N.J.

ORACLE manuals:

"ORACLE RDBMS with the Transaction Processing Subsystem," March 1988, Version 6.0.

"ORACLE for DEC VAX/VMS Installation and User's Guide," ORACLE Part No 1001.

"ORACLE for IBM VM/SP Installation and User's Guide," ORACLE Part No 1003.

"ORACLE for Sequent/Unix Installation and User's Guide," ORACLE Part No 1008.

"ORACLE ERROR MESSAGES and Codes," ORACLE Part No 3605.

"ORACLE Utilities User's Guide," ORACLE Part No 3602.

Perkinson, R. (1985). *Data Analysis—The Key to Data Base Design*, QED Information Sciences, Inc., Wellesley, Mass.

Wiederhold, G. (1977). *Database Design*, McGraw-Hill, New York.

Zloof, M. (1976). "Operations on Hierarchical Data Bases," *Proc. NCC* 45.

Glossary

access. The operation of seeking, reading, or writing data on a storage unit.

access method. A technique used to transfer a physical record from or to a mass storage device.

access pattern. The general sequence in which the data structure is accessed—i.e., from tuple to tuple, from segment to segment, etc.

access time. The time interval between the instant when an instruction control unit initiates a call for data and the instant when delivery of the data is completed from the device control unit.

address. An identification (number, name, label) for a location in which data is stored.

addressing. The means of assigning data to storage locations, and subsequent retrieval, on the basis of the key of the data.

algorithm. A set of statements to solve a problem in a finite number of steps.

alias. An alternate label used to refer to a data element.

application blocking of data. The grouping of different occurrences of the same type of data by the application programmer. The application programmer takes care of data placement, location, deletion, overflow, etc.

archival data base. A data base copy saved for historical, recovery, or restoration purposes.

association. A relationship between two entities that is represented in a data model.

atomic. The smallest addressable unit within a system.

atomic-level data. Archival (time-variant) data at a low level of detail with a moderate probability of access positioned to serve as a foundation for dss processing.

attribute. A property that can assume values for entities or relationships. Entities can be assigned several attributes (e.g., a tuple in a relation consists of values). Some systems also allow relationships to have attributes.

audit trail. Data that is available to trace activity; typically used for data base transactions or for terminal activity.

availability. A measure of the reliability of a system, indicating the fraction of time when the system is available divided by the amount of time the system should be available.

B Tree.* a type of indexing algorithm used to create and store indexes.

backup. To restore the data base to its state at a previous point in time. Backup is often achieved from an archival data base— that is, a snapshot of the data base at a specified time.

batch. Computer environment in which (usually long-running and sequentially oriented) programs exclusively access data and user activity is not interactive.

batch environment. A sequentially dominated mode of processing. In batch, input is collected and batched for future processing throughout the day. Once collected, the batch input is transacted sequentially against one or more data bases.

batch window. The time when the online system is available for batch or sequential processing. The batch window occurs during nonpeak processing hours.

bill of materials. A listing of the materials used in a manufacturing process. The structure of how the materials are used in the manufacturing process can be derived from the bill of materials.

bind. To assign a value to a data element, variable, or parameter; the attachment of a data definition to a program prior to execution of the program.

block. A basic unit of data structuring; the physical unit of transport and storage; sometimes called a page. A block contains one or more records.

blocking. The combining of two or more physical records so that they are jointly read or written by one machine instruction.

block splitting. A data management activity that allows a fully packed block to be split into two or more blocks, where each new block contains some free space.

buffer. An area of storage that holds data temporarily while it is being received, transmitted, read, or written. It is often used to compensate for differences in the speed or timing of devices. Buffers are used in terminals, peripheral devices, storage units, and in the CPU.

checkpoint. An identified snapshot of the data base or a point at which the transitions have been frozen or are quiescent.

checkpoint/restart. A means of restarting a program at some point other than the beginning, used after a failure or interruption has occurred. *N* checkpoints may be used at intervals throughout an application program; at these points records are written giving enough information about the status of the program to permit its being restarted at that point.

claimed block. A second or subsequent physical block designated to store table data when the originally allocated block has run out of space.

cluster. A means of storing together data from multiple tables on the basis of a common key value.

cluster key. The key around which the cluster is built.

code. (1) To represent data or a computer program in a form that can be accepted by a data processor. (2) To transform data so that it cannot be understood by anyone who does not have the algorithm to decode the data before its presentation.

column. A vertical table cut in which values are selected from the same domain. The column is named in the heads.

commit. A condition issued by a group of operators or transactions when the changes to a data base are concluded satisfactorily and can no longer be cancelled or rolled back, except as a whole by a later special command to undo the entire group.

compaction. A technique for reducing the number of bits required for storage without destroying any information content.

concatenated index. An index over multiple columns.

connector. A symbol used to indicate that one occurrence of data has a relationship with another occurrence of data. Connectors are used in conceptual data base design.

control data base. A data base containing data other than that directly related to the function of the application. Typical control data bases are terminal data bases, security data bases, audit data bases, table data bases, etc. Although control data bases are necessary, it is mandatory that they be implemented properly, as opposed to an ORACLE control data base.

cursor. An indicator that designates a current position relative to the ordering of the rows in a table and is open for the duration of a session.

DASD. Direct-access storage device.

data. A recording of facts, concepts, or instructions on a storage medium for communication, retrieval, and processing by automatic means and presentation as information that is understandable to humans.

data administrator. The individual who manages organizational data and is responsible for the specification, acquisition, and maintenance of the data management software and the design, validation, and security of the files or data base.

data definition language (DDL). (also called a *data description language*) The language used to define the data base schema and give additional data that allows the DBMS to generate the internal tables, indexes, buffers, and storage criteria necessary for data base processing.

data description language (DDL). A language for describing data (in some software for describing the logical rather than the physical data; in other software, for both).

data dictionary system. A software tool that allows the recording, storing, and processing of such metadata as definitions, descriptions, and relationships between programs, data, and users.

data-driven process. A process whose resource utilization depends on the structure and occurrences of the data being operated on. For example, a hierarchical root has, on the average, 2 dependents, but has one case where there are 1000 dependents. Any process accessing the root and all dependents will be data driven (i.e., behaving nicely 99 percent of the time and awkwardly 1 percent of the time).

data element. An attribute of an entity; a uniquely named and well-defined category of data that consists of data items and that is included in a record of an activity.

data manipulation language (DML). A programming language that is supported by a DBMS and used to access a data base; language constructs for addition to higher-order language (e.g., COBOL) for the purpose of data base manipulation.

data model. (1) The logical data structures, including operations and constraints, provided by a DBMS for effective data base processing. (2) The system used for data representation (e.g., the ERA or relational model).

DBMS Language Interface (DB I/O Module). Software that applications call which, in turn, calls the DBMS. By making the interface to the DBMS indirect, several benefits are derived, such as standards enforcement, standard error checks, and so on.

deadly embrace. The event in which transaction A desires to get at data protected by transaction B, when, at the same time, transaction B desires to get at data protected by transaction A. Processing comes to a halt until either A or B is given access to data.

decompaction. The opposite of compaction. Data is stored in a compacted form, but must be decompacted upon use to make sense to the user.

decryption. The opposite of encryption. Data is stored in an encrypted form and must be decrypted upon use to make sense to the user.

derived data. Data about multiple customers or multiple events.

derived data element. A data element that is not necessarily stored but that can be generated when needed (e.g., the age given the date of birth and current date).

direct access. Retrieval or storage of data by a reference to its location on a volume, rather than relative to the previously retrieved or stored data. The access mechanism goes directly to the data in question, as is normally required with online use of data.

direct-access storage device (DASD). A data storage unit on which data can be accessed directly and randomly without having to progress through a serial file such as tape. A disk unit is a direct-access storage device.

directory. A table giving the relationships between items of data; sometimes a table (index) giving the addresses of data.

dss data (decision support systems). Data used in a free-form fashion to support managerial decisions.

encoding. A shortening or abbreviation of the physical representation of a data value. For example, male = M, female = F.

encryption. The transformation of data by means of an algorithm from one form to another so that the data is unrecognizable in its transformed representation. Encryption is done for security reasons. Should an unauthorized person stumble on the transformed data, the data would be useless without the transformation algorithm.

entity. A person, place, event, or thing of interest to users at the highest level of abstraction.

entity-relationship diagram (ERD). A high-level schematic of data at its highest level of abstraction.

foreign key. An attribute that is not a primary key to a relation in a relational system, but whose values are values of the primary key of another relation's tuples.

format. The arrangement or layout of data in or on a data medium (i.e., buffer) or in a program definition.

heuristics. A method of obtaining a solution through inference or trial and error that uses approximate methods while evaluating the progress toward an acceptable goal.

index. The portion of the storage structure maintained to provide efficient access to a record when its index key item value is known.

instance. A member of a shared partition data base system, as in an ORACLE cluster run in MVS CICS.

interactive. A mode of processing combining some aspects of online processing and some aspects of batch processing. In interactive processing, the user can directly interact with data over which the user has exclusive control. In addition, the user can cause sequential activity to occur on the data.

intersection data. Data that is associated with the conjunction of two or more entities or record types.

I/O (input/output). The means by which data is stored on DASD. I/O is measured in milliseconds, while computer processing is measured in nanoseconds.

join. An operation that takes two relations as operands and produces a new relation by concatenating the tuples and matching the corresponding columns when a stated condition holds between the two.

key. A data item or combination of data items used to identify or locate a record instance (or other data grouping).

key, primary. A key that is used to uniquely identify a record instance (or other data grouping).

key, secondary. A key that does not uniquely identify a record instance; that is, more than one record instance can have the same key value.

line. The hardware by which data flows to or from the processor; typically, lines go to terminals, printers, other processors, etc.

line time. The amount of time required for a transaction to go either from the terminal to the processor or from the processor to the terminal. Typically, line time is the single largest component of online response time.

living sample. A representative data base, typically used for analytical work in the face of a very large data base. Periodically, the very large data base is stripped of data so that the living sample represents a cross section of the large data base. Then statistical activity can be done against the living sample data base without disturbing the large data base.

load. To insert data values into a data base that was previously empty.

loading. The automatic recording of data concerning attempts to query, load, augment, or update the data base.

lockup. The event that occurs when a data base is being used exclusively and other programs desire to access the data base but cannot.

magnetic tape. The medium most closely associated with sequential processing; a large ribbon on which magnetic images are stored and retrieved.

master file. A concept from sequential processing in which a given file holds the definitive data for a given system.

message. The data input by the user in the online environment that is used to drive a transaction, or the data that is output to the user as a result of the execution of a transaction.

MTAR (maximum transaction arrival rate). The peak rate at which transactions arrive for data base processing.

normal forms.

first normal form. Data that has been organized into two-dimensional flat files without repeating groups.

second normal form. Data that functionally depends on the entire candidate key.

third normal form. Data that has had all transitive dependencies on other data items within the record removed, except for the candidate key.

fourth normal form. Data whose candidate key is related to all data items in the record and that contains no more than one nontrivial multivalued dependency on the candidate key.

natural join. A join in which the redundant tuple components generated by the join are removed.

navigate. To steer a course through a data base by using such devices as indexes and pointers to arrive at and examine a record and data item values.

nine's complement. Transformation of a numeric field calculated by subtracting its value from a value greater than or equal to the field consisting digitally of all nines.

normalize. To decompose complex data structures into normal form structures.

null. An item or record for which no value currently exists or may ever exist.

numeric. A representation using only numbers and the decimal point.

online storage. Storage devices, especially the storage media they contain, under the direct control of a computing system, not offline or in a volume library.

operating system. Software that enables a computer to supervise its own operations, automatically calling in programs, routines, language, and data as needed for continuous throughput of different types of jobs.

operational data. Data used to support the day-to-day operations of an organization, usually at a detailed level.

operations. The organizational unit responsible for making the computer environment operable.

overflow. The condition in which a record (or segment) cannot be stored in its home address, that is, the storage location logically assigned to it on loading. It may be stored in a special overflow location, or in the home address of other records; the area of DASD where data is sent when collisions occur or records go when they need to be written and there is no space in primary DASD.

page fixed. In a virtual environment, when programs or data are defined so that they cannot be removed from main storage, they are said to be page fixed. Only a limited amount of storage can be page fixed.

page fault. A program interruption that occurs when a page that is referred to is not in main memory and has to be read in.

paging. In virtual storage systems, the technique of making memory appear larger than it is by transferring blocks (pages) of data or programs into that memory from external storage when they are needed.

parallel data organizations. Organizations that permit multiple access arms to search, read, or write data simultaneously.

parallel I/O. In a nonmainframe environment, the situation in which more than one processor does I/O.

parallel search storage. A storage device in which one or more parts of all storage locations are queried simultaneously for a certain condition.

parameter. An elementary data item or an array of data items that specifies the data type of its values and assumes or supplies the value(s) of the corresponding argument in the call of a procedure.

parsing. The algorithm that translates syntax into meaningful machine instructions. Parsing determines the meaning of the statements issued in the data manipulation language.

PCTFREE. An option that allows space to be preserved in a block for update processing.

PCTUSED. An option that describes how much data the designer would like to see used in the block.

peak period. Time (day, month, etc.) when the system experiences the greatest volume of transactions or activity.

populate. To place occurrences of data values into a previously empty data base. See also *load.*

precision. The degree of discrimination with which a quantity is stated. For example, a three-digit numeral discriminates among 1000 possibilities from 000 to 999.

primary key. An item whose value uniquely identifies a record or tuple.

processor. The hardware at the center of processing. Processors are divided into three categories: mainframes, minicomputers, and microcomputers.

processor cycles. The hardware internal cycles that do many functions that drive the computer, such as initiate I/O, perform logic, move data, and perform arithmetic functions.

projection. An operation that takes one relation as an operand and returns a second relation that consists of only the selected attributes columns, with duplicate rows eliminated.

purge date. The date on or after which a storage area is available to be overwritten. Used in conjunction with a file label, it is a means of protecting file data until an agreed release date is reached.

queue time. The amount of time a transaction takes after being transmitted to the processor and before going into execution. Queue time is dependent on many factors: the system load, the level of integrity, the priority of the transaction, etc. Queue time can become the largest factor in poor online response time.

query language. A language that enables a user to interact directly with a DBMS to retrieve and possibly modify its data.

random access. To obtain data directly from any storage location regardless of its position with respect to the previously referenced information. Also called *direct access.*

random-access storage. A storage technique in which the time required to obtain information is independent of the location of the information most recently obtained. This strict definition must be qualified by the observation that we usually mean relatively random. Thus magnetic drums are relatively nonrandom access when compared to magnetic cores for main memory, but relatively random access when compared to magnetic tapes for file storage.

record. An aggregation of values of data items or elements.

record-at-a-time processing. Access of data a unit at a time (i.e., a record at a time, a tuple at a time, etc.)

record type. The category to which a record instance belongs, as defined by the record format in the data base schema.

recovery. The restoration of the data base to an original position or prior condition, often after major damage to the physical medium. See also *commit.*

recursion. The definition of something in terms of itself. For example, a bill of materials is usually defined in terms of itself.

relational algebra. A language providing a set of Boolean and other operators for manipulating relations.

relational calculus. A language that states the desired results of a relational data base manipulation using first-order predicate calculus.

relational model. A data model allowing the expression of relationships among data elements as mathematical relations. The relation is a table of data representing occurrences of the relationship as the rows (i.e., tuples).

reorganization. The process of unloading data (in a poorly organized state) and reloading (into a well-organized state). Reorganization in some DBMS is also done to restructure the data base.

repeating group. A collection of data that can occur several times within a given record occurrence.

response time (user). The amount of time the user has to wait from the time a transaction is entered until a response is returned. Response time is a function of communication line time, processing time, and amount of processing activity.

row. A nonempty sequence of values in a table and the smallest unit of data that can be stored in and erased from a table.

row ID. A pseudo column for every row, which contains the address of the row.

scope of integration. The formal English language definition of the boundaries of the system.

secondary index. An index composed of secondary keys rather than primary keys.

secondary key. An attribute that is not the primary or ordering key but for which an index is maintained.

secondary storage. Storage facilities that are not an integral part of the computer but directly linked to and controlled by the computer (e.g., disks, magnetic tapes, etc.).

security. The protection provided to prevent unauthorized or accidental access to a data base or its elements; the updating, copying, removal, or destruction of the data base; or the changing or running of a proscribed application.

select. To identify a subset of stored data that meets specified criteria.

set. A number of distinct objects with membership criteria. In a network- or CODASYL-type data base, a set is a named logical relationship between record types, consisting of one owner record type, one or more member record types, and a prescribed order among the instances of member records.

set-at-a-time processing. Access of data by groups of data, each member of which satisfies some selection criteria.

snapshot. A data base dump or archiving of data at a given time.

sort. To arrange a file in sequence by a specified key.

SQL. ("see-qwell") A language used in relational processing

standard work unit. (SWU) The amount of processing done by a transaction in accordance with a predefined limit (usually measured in terms of I/Os).

subject data base. A data base and related system designed to support business functions and their applications by managing the data for a particular subject area.

subject data base. A collection of like data relevant to the enterprise.

syntax. The rules governing the structure of expressions or sentences in a language.

system log. An audit trail of relevant system happenings, such as transaction entries, data base changes, etc.

system of record. The final authority as to the accuracy of data. By definition, the system of record is correct; there can be only one system of record.

table. A relation that consists of a set of columns with a heading and a set of rows (i.e., tuples).

transaction. A command, message, or input record that explicitly or implicitly calls for a processing action (e.g., updating a file). A transaction is atomic with respect to recovery and concurrency.

tuple. A group of related fields in a row of a relation; a row of the relation or table.

update. To change values in all or selected entries, groups, or data items stored in a data base; to add or delete data occurrences of their relationships.

user. A person or process issuing commands and messages to the information system.

variable-length columns. Columns where length varies.

view. An external relation that consists of attributes retrieved or derived from one or more base relations, joined and projected as given in the view definition.

Answers to Chapter Questions

CHAPTER 1 ORACLE—AN OVERVIEW

1. a
2. a; b; d
3. an index
4. the entire
5. e; c
6. may not
7. name; physical attribute
8. true
9. may not
10. All listed
11. false
12. 255
13. fixed point; floating point
14. precision; scale
15. seven
16. 65,535
17. cannot

18. any
19. true
20. one
21. true
22. rows
23. true
24. false
25. false
26. table
27. dba; data base administrator
28. may be
29. a; c
30. true
31. may be
32. may not
33. a; c
34. c
35. false
36. loading; maintenance
37. two; three
38. a
39. anywhere, in a particular location
40. e
41. all
42. usually bad
43. application
44. fewer
45. true

CHAPTER 2 ORACLE—MORE BASICS

1. false
2. primary; secondary
3. unique

4. index
5. concatenated
6. false
7. like
8. efficient
9. b
10. a;b;c;d
11. PCTFREE; PCTUSED
12. I/O
13. mechanical
14. two; three
15. virtual (or logical); physical
16. false—virtual I/O is not slow
17. should not
18. online processing; batch window
19. many small transactions
20. large programs using many resources
21. long-running programs
22. utilities
23. 6:00–7:00 p.m.; 5:00–6:00 a.m.
24. reorganization; recovery; loading; monitoring
25. some
26. 1:n; m:n; reclusive
27. foreign key
28. 1:n
29. confusion, complexity
30. cross-reference
31. itself
32. cross reference tables
33. operational; dss or decision support
34. under most circumstances should not
35. detail, summary, repetitive processing, heuristic processing, clerical, managerial, etc.
36. an ORACLE environment

37. a subset/superset of data
38. may
39. should not

CHAPTER 3 CONCEPTUAL DATA BASE DESIGN—NORMALIZATION

1. logical data base design; physical data base design
2. Logical (conceptual) data base design
3. are many
4. data
5. process model
6. corporate
7. true
8. is sometimes
9. primitive; derived
10. true
11. primitive
12. interview; previous models; the corporate data model; reports; screens; etc.
13. a high-level; mid-level
14. ERD; subject areas
15. keys (primary); activities; groups of data; connectors; "type of data"; multiple occurrences of data; secondary keys
16. existence dependency criteria
17. do
18. false—foreign key data is necessarily redundant
19. frequency of access; volume of data; growth pattern
20. is not
21. is
22. functional decomposition; data flow diagrams; mini specs; state transaction diagrams

CHAPTER 4 CONCEPTUAL DATA BASE DESIGN—DENORMALIZATION

1. relational
2. nonkey; key (in this order)
3. many
4. dispersed, distributed, scattered
5. dynamically
6. apply
7. do not imply
8. data
9. table
10. always
11. common, like
12. occurrence
13. no
14. true
15. buffer
16. high
17. clustered
18. clustering
19. never under any conditions
20. may be
21. redundancy
22. update
23. stable
24. changes
25. first
26. all
27. depends on
28. much
29. clustering

CHAPTER 5 PHYSICAL DATA BASE DESIGN IN ORACLE

1. directly
2. sequentially
3. small
4. large
5. two
6. references, index entries, index references
7. maintenance
8. index
9. many
10. referential integrity
11. application, application programmer
12. may
13. false
14. batch
15. reorganization
16. recovery, reorganization
17. reducing
18. does not necessarily imply
19. enhances
20. true
21. removed
22. key
23. geography, random values, line of business, marketing classifications, etc.
24. only a few
25. many, all, most
26. index
27. one or more
28. should not
29. will not
30. always
31. both are correct

32. true
33. true
34. fewer
35. saved
36. physical block size, block size—number of occurrences of data—pattern of access, access pattern—pattern of insertions/deletions
37. false
38. unknown
39. may not
40. single record searches, massive manipulation
41. much
42. lowest
43. slower
44. variable-length field
45. are not
46. true
47. is not
48. wasted
49. after
50. will help but not solve
51. PCTFREE
52. page
53. control
54. terminal, security, audit, tables, variables
55. enqueue, enqueuing, locking, deadlock, deadly embrace
56. update
57. true
58. c
59. true
60. may
61. one
62. true
63. b
64. recovery; reorganization

65. recovered
66. true
67. internal cleanliness of data, changing index structure, changing row structure
68. unavailable
69. longer
70. should be
71. partitioning
72. system; application
73. some
74. will not
75. may cost; may save (either is correct)
76. symbolic, representative
77. true
78. saves, prevents, minimizes
79. usage of data, size of data, variability of data size, many answers

CHAPTER 6 HIGH AVAILABILITY

1. length; frequency
2. quantifiable, measurable
3. recovery; reorganization
4. is
5. is not
6. reduce, shrink
7. unload/reload
8. three
9. discovery
10. is not
11. diagnostic
12. true
13. formulated, laid, outlined
14. is
15. true
16. large

17. prescriptive
18. is
19. two and three
20. two and three
21. two
22. internal; redefine
23. true
24. is not
25. size; structure
26. row size, overhead, freespace, free pages, index space
27. levels
28. maximum
29. target
30. prototype
31. false
32. probability
33. record
34. necessary
35. expensive
36. expensive
37. does not mean
38. expensive, automatic
39. slower
40. primitive; derived
41. large, excessive
42. administrative
43. is not
44. true
45. applications
46. key
47. must
48. processors
49. *n*, an indefinite number of, an indeterminate number of
50. application

51. false
52. independently
53. false
54. may
55. will not

CHAPTER 7 ORACLE TRANSACTION DESIGN

1. establishment
2. are not
3. both
4. does not modify
5. true
6. should not
7. a
8. enqueue
9. enqueued
10. longer
11. b
12. electronic
13. milli
14. nano
15. true
16. is not
17. is not
18. is
19. recognized
20. late
21. batch
22. unfriendly
23. buffers, data, network, internal protection, etc.
24. data-
25. operates, executes, runs, etc.
26. b

27. excessive, large, huge, monstrous, not worth it, etc.
28. designed
29. undesigned
30. small, limited, etc.
31. true
32. function, purpose, use
33. iterate, repeat
34. false
35. true
36. true
37. true
38. false
39. false
40. true
41. true
42. false
43. true

CHAPTER 8 THE ORACLE BATCH ENVIRONMENT

1. batch
2. batch
3. always
4. true
5. true
6. substantially
7. entire batch environment
8. true
9. the same
10. the same
11. utilities, batched updates, extracts, system software, undesigned transactions
12. false
13. often

14. is not
15. separate, different, unique, etc.
16. extract
17. individual
18. single
19. extra runs, more extracts, etc.
20. a
21. must
22. usually
23. prioritized
24. month-; year-
25. true

CHAPTER 9 ARCHIVAL PROCESSING AND ORACLE

1. does not
2. archival data is not updated; operational data is able to be updated.
3. are not
4. more
5. heuristic
6. profound
7. microfiche, magnetic tape, DASD
8. electronic reproducible; electronic nonreproducible
9. more
10. more
11. primitive
12. can
13. because archival processing involves unknown future requirements
14. format, structure
15. codes
16. subjects
17. index
18. true

19. subset
20. true
21. searching for specific records
22. very appropriate
23. time stamped
24. unit of time
25. a discrete organization of data; a continuous organization of data
26. true

CHAPTER 10 EXTRACT PROCESSING IN ORACLE

1. simple
2. e
3. b
4. DASD, disk storage, storage
5. application programs
6. parameters, values
7. operational, production
8. index
9. output file
10. summarized; consolidated, merged
11. report; decision support analysis; trend analysis; demographic analysis; exception reporting.
12. transformation
13. true
14. should not
15. should not
16. is
17. bulk, bulk storage
18. expensive, awkward, not easy to do, slow
19. expensive, wasteful
20. detail, summarization
21. extracted
22. consolidated, summarized, reordered

23. highest
24. usage
25. does not
26. does
27. a modest amount, a small amount, a manageable amount
28. separate, split
29. scan, selection, extract; load
30. CPU
31. consolidate
32. true
33. sequentially
34. changed, been altered, been updated, created
35. more
36. more
37. an important
38. an index, indexing
39. time, I/O; DASD, disk storage
40. application; system, DBMS, data base
41. does
42. false
43. application
44. reduce
45. increases
46. false
47. true
48. background
49. small
50. I/O space, DASD, disk storage
51. true
52. reduces dramatically
53. implies
54. should not
55. is

CHAPTER 11 TESTING ORACLE PRODUCTION SYSTEMS

Section I

1. is
2. more
3. coding, logic, algorithms, resource consumption, performance
4. false
5. new; existing
6. input used to drive the test environment; data bases on which testing is done; configuration of the teleprocessing monitor and DBMS
7. must be
8. stress
9. all
10. bringing down, killing, abending
11. interrelationships, relationships
12. small
13. reinitialized
14. are not
15. all (a,b,c,d,e)
16. may
17. execute the test input against live data
18. created
19. 10 percent
20. "hot spots," bottlenecks
21. true
22. 25 percent
23. false
24. I/O, data base calls
25. set-at-a-time
26. variable, volatile
27. total, complete
28. teleprocessing monitor; data base management system

29. response time; queue lengths; arrival rates
30. should
31. all (a,b,c,d,e)
32. 10 percent, one-tenth
33. may
34. shutdown
35. joins
36. arithmetically
37. generate, issue, create
38. teleprocessing monitor; data base management system monitor
39. damaging, disturbing, harming
40. two
41. preliminary
42. program logic, the first few tests run
43. reinitialized
44. 10 percent
45. one full set
46. is not
47. may not
48. set
49. 30 to 45
50. should
51. maximum
52. preliminary
53. true
54. larger, community
55. many, lots of
56. test log
57. date of test; who conducted test; what data was altered
58. creating tables; granting/revoking authority; creating restore utilities; monitor size/usage of test data; moving table definitions from test to production; monitoring/administering naming conventions.

Section II

1. affects
2. know, predetermine
3. reset, reinitialize
4. data base administrator, project manager
5. many, multiple, more than one
6. driver
7. may
8. remove, takeout, disable
9. flow, sequence
10. dumps of test data bases; screen transmissions; reports; memory dumps; debug comments; monitor output, etc.
11. paths
12. true
13. should
14. true
15. force
16. false
17. delete; update
18. true
19. range, edit range
20. referential integrity
21. true
22. false (This may or may not be true)
23. independent
24. the same
25. I/O Module
26. error module
27. simulation
28. foreign key, referential integrity
29. recursive
30. may be able to
31. may not
32. false

33. precompiler; compiler; dumps; source listing; JCL listings; application program output; data base management system/teleprocessing monitor output

34. stress

35. full

36. multiple, many, more than one

37. how many resources, what resources, what consumption

38. displayed, written out

39. joins

Index

P

Q

R